The Diamond Effect:

How inspiring leaders change the world

By: Tony Dixon

Copyright

Book cover art design by Jason Trias Reyes

See more about Jason Reyes at stufficreate.com

For more information about Tony Dixon go to leadthruinspiration.com

Tony can be reached by email at: leadthruinspiration@gmail.com

Connect on LinkedIn
Follow @InspiredLdshp

Table of Contents

]

Introduction

Great leaders come by from time to time. We see them in every walk of life inspiring others with their amazing example of humanity, courage, resolve and heroism. At times they appear to come out of nowhere, arriving on the scene just when they are needed most as a beacon of light, of hope. Inspiring leaders are compelled with optimism. They are knocked down, arrested, beaten, shot, shamed and told to stop. Yet faced with what others would consider insurmountable challenges, these individuals choose not to simply speak, write, protest or fight, but to live the whole of their lives for a cause.

Inspiration comes not from people alone. Inspiration is looking around and realizing we don't know everything about what is here much less what is out there. Inspiration stares back at you when gazing at the night sky in all of its glory. Inspiration is what drives people to work together in order to solve the great challenges our planet presents us. Inspiration is and forever will be something deeply personal that resonates with the emotions serving as a constant reminder that even though we are human, we can achieve the inhuman if we sufficiently commit ourselves.

You will find at different points throughout this book that there are questions that I provide an answer, but there are also questions for you to answer. These questions are intended to stimulate thought about the most important ideas this book raises and are denoted by the letters **RQ.** Leadership becomes very messy when you try to create definitions. It is important however, to take some time and think about your own ideas and beliefs as they relate to the topics in this book. Don't worry, there is no test at the end!

Mother to Son

"Well, son, I'll tell you:
Life for me ain't been no crystal stair.
It's had tacks in it,
And splinters,
And boards torn up,
And places with no carpet on the floor --
Bare.
But all the time
I'se been a-climbin' on,
And reachin' landin's,
And turnin' corners,
And sometimes goin' in the dark
Where there ain't been no light.
So boy, don't you turn back.
Don't you set down on the steps
'Cause you finds it's kinder hard.
Don't you fall now --
For I'se still goin', honey,
I'se still climbin',
And life for me ain't been no crystal stair."

— Langston Hughes, 1922

1. Everything this book is about

What is The Diamond Effect?

Diamonds are considered beautiful and highly valuable; yet, all diamonds first start out as carbon. Only through intense pressure can carbon transform from an inexpensive black piece of material into one of the most sought after and highly valued stones in human culture.

Diamonds are found naturally in a number of colors such as blue, yellow, brown, red, pink, green, purple, and orange just as people are found in many different shades and backgrounds. Diamonds are so renowned for their strength that they are used in high powered diamond tipped cutting instruments and a number of other applications beside jewelry. Certain leaders are relied upon for their own sense of personal strength of character and resolve.

What exactly is the Diamond Effect? It is a relentless focus on a unifying sense of purpose; the ability to overcome immense pressures in order to transform from one's original composition into something much greater; the strength to set out daring goals and then achieve them. This is The Diamond Effect. Continually organizations recognize that a culture of leadership through inspiration is more desired than one of excessive rules, bureaucracy, coercive motivational techniques and many of the other practices that have belabored groups causing a lack of performance and morale.

People who serve in organizations want to be led by a diamond leader. The person who stands out, not because of an extravagant lifestyle, but an extravagance in caring about the lives they touch. Diamond leaders make themselves vulnerable by being completely honest with followers; though often choosing to find a positive light to see in even the most challenging of situations.

The most inspiring people that are found in society are examples of overcoming great challenges. Working constantly led with a sense of passion and purpose, these individuals made their own transformation from a simpler version of themselves into the diamonds they would become that would inspire many others.

The purpose of this book is to stimulate thought about the ideas presented and to challenge the reader to embrace a lifestyle based on inspirational leadership. It is the hope that you, the reader, will see this as a type of how to guide for understanding leadership through inspiration that has the potential to truly revolutionize the way organizations are led out of a rethinking of its sense of purpose.

The problem with inspiration

Inspiration is not a simple definition to lay out. When doing research into the definition or to try to find a working definition that describes inspiration, one can be a bit discouraged that no such thing really exists. A great deal of this controversy over something that at first glance doesn't seem as though it should be so difficult is thanks to the fact that inspiration is a subjective term defined differently by many people. It is more difficult because what inspires one does not inspire others. Inspiration is an abstract concept that people can describe the tangible effects of, but cannot put them together to give a definitive answer.

If you were to ask someone to describe inspiration you may hear something like this: "something that creates excitement" or "something that makes you want to do something." The problem is that when put to the test these answers fail to hold up on their own. Let's look at something that creates excitement. A roller coaster creates excitement in people; but would you say that a roller coaster really inspires you? Perhaps it does. Or how about the answer of something that makes you want to do something. When your stomach begins to rumble you know it is time to eat. Is the hungry feeling in your stomach inspiring you at that moment or is it simply a signal sent to your brain telling you to go find the nearest food and eat? Instead I prefer to think of inspiration as "Something that moves you."

You see, inspiration *does* contain these elements. Inspiration contains other elements as well and they are not necessarily used all at once. It is also true that what inspires some does not inspire all. The 2012 United States Presidential election saw Barack Obama re-elected to a second term with only 51% of voters picking him. Clearly what inspired some to vote for him did not catch on with all people. This is in large part because people share different values from one another. This is also why a democratic system can work well since it allows for the leadership ideally to represent the values and beliefs of the majority of people at a given time. The same is true in business. Consumers vote with their wallets. The Apple iPod is an mp3 player but no one calls it an mp3 player. And if you asked people to mention other mp3 players most would not be able to. They might at best guess at other companies that make mp3 players.

What is inspiration?

Merriam-Webster provides a number of definitions for the word inspiration. For the purpose of understanding it in the context of inspirational leadership we will use the following: the action or power of moving the intellect or emotions; the act of influencing or suggesting opinions.

The first clause of the definition is a fairly accurate way of describing inspiration. When the definition is tested with known examples of inspirational people or events like that of Jesus of Nazareth, it is obvious that his life and teachings as a religious, moral and spiritual leader had the power of moving the intellect or emotions as it still does today. The recent string of mass shootings has moved both the intellect and emotions of the populace to make changes to the way that issues such as school safety, public health and firearm regulation are dealt with.

The second clause of the definition has more to do with leadership though not completely an answer to the question, "what is inspiration?" Opinions can be influenced or suggested through bribes or uses of force. By testing the definition it becomes clear that being able to influence or suggest opinion is not altogether inspirational. Someone holding a gun to your head is able to influence your opinion of what to do in that moment, although you are not being inspired per se. However, being able to influence or suggest opinions is essential to leadership.

In the end, since inspiration is a quality, it can mean something different from person to person. Therefore the definition of what inspiration is can also be different for different people. With that in mind, you can choose to use the definition just described or use your own. You may find that your definition changes as you learn more about inspiration. This book will hopefully provoke thinking and cause you to discover new ways to think of a powerful force that can be seen every day. Not only can it be seen, it can be transformed into something useable that becomes an empowering tool for anyone that chooses to accept it.

What is leadership?

Leadership is a difficult word to define because it is subjective and abstract. You can count seven pennies and know that you have seven. You may argue that a penny is worth less than the metal it is composed of, but nevertheless you have seven pennies. For leadership there are literally thousands of definitions, none of which everyone agrees upon.

Part of the problem is that our view of what leadership is has evolved over the years. There was a time when people believed that you had to be born a leader. People also moved to the idea of believing that a leader possessed certain traits like sociability, intelligence and charisma. Military leadership has provided a certain lens by which to view leadership in addition to several other theories which has taken us through the industrial age. There is situational leadership, servant leadership, transformational leadership and others. Now we have leadership in the post industrial, globalized, and technologically interconnected 21st century. These factors make leadership all the more complex and difficult to understand.

Today many people hold the belief that leadership requires a certain level of ethics and therefore do not consider people like Adolf Hitler or Moammar Khaddafi to have practiced leadership even though both were in positions of formal authority as leaders of a country. I have difficulty agreeing with this notion because even if you believe something is bad leadership or unethical leadership, I find it hard to say it is not leadership at all. Because if it is not leadership, then what is it? For the purpose of this book, leadership is defined as the act of leading. It is clearly a simplified version that approaches the concept of leadership in its most basic form.

What is inspirational leadership?

Inspirational leadership is when a person uses the elements of inspiration and then combines them with the intangible elements of leadership. Combining the ideas of inspiration with leadership we arrive at inspirational leadership. Broken down according to the above mentioned definitions, inspirational leadership is the act of leading in such a way that influences emotion and opinion. Therefore, inspirational leadership is using the elements of inspiration in order to get others to follow you.

Leadership is seen through many lenses. One can look at leadership in terms of traits a person possesses that allows them to be a leader like charisma, intelligence, sociability, openness or confidence while others look at style or situation. Each one has a place in the quest to understand leadership. There is leadership used during change, leadership during crisis, situational leadership, day to day leadership and many others that will not be mentioned now. Inspirational leadership will be explained much more in the next chapter with several different examples to help make it more clear.

One thing that is certain is that the young people of Generation Y are increasingly uninterested in working for a leader or organization that is uninspiring. As people become more socially conscious, they want to work for an organization that aligns with their own personal values and work with a leader that supports an inspirational approach. When the U.S. economy was based in farming and then later based in industrial age work such as manufacturing, the nature of the work was by and large repetitive and unexciting. People would work at the same factory for thirty or forty years then retire. Now it is common for people to not only change jobs more often but also industries. The combination of globalization and technological advances has pushed people to be more adaptive to change or otherwise risk falling behind. Because of this ever changing landscape, workers virtually demand that their leadership and organization be just as cutting edge and adaptive. As the global environment moves further toward an information and connection stage, the need for management methods popular in the manufacturing age become less appealing and overall less effective as they drive people away who feel they are under a more rigid command and control system and not one of openness and equality.

Why is it important to distinguish inspiration from inspirational leadership?

It is important to make the distinction because if the inspiration is not taken in an intentioned direction with a desired purpose or end result then there is no leadership involved. Nature inspires many people to stare up at the night sky in wonder. Painters, scientists, writers, the ancient Egyptians and many others have been inspired by that same sky. However, the sky never directed those individuals on how to materialize the inspiration. The sky only provides a source just as the Sun provides a source of heat yet does not tell lead people to make solar panels or anything else that may be created or thought of as a result of the Sun.

Why inspirational leadership and not inspirational management?

Leadership is what people desire above management. People prefer extra leadership over extra management. Nobody asks their boss to be less open to new ideas or to disconnect with the vision and values of the organization. No one asks their boss instead to write more policies and rules in exchange for vision and mentorship. Humans inherently recognize the superiority of leadership over management by choosing to publicly recognize the ones who do an exceptional job at leading. Why do people talk about the likes of Abraham Lincoln, Nelson Mandela or Mohandas Gandhi with a sense of reverence? Is it because they were able to get people to follow the rules? Was it because they were great at writing a policy manual or creating a comprehensive incentive structure to meet strategic objectives?

The answer is obviously NO! People that follow a particular leader for any reason, be it that they work for a company, support a social cause or a political party want to feel as though the leader connects with them personally via mutually held beliefs and values. Leaders who inspire understand the need to focus on something higher than just spreadsheets and reports. It is about the vision.

For this reason, people do not celebrate the many Wall Street bankers who make millions of dollars by pushing buttons playing with other people's money. Even when the result of their efforts are positive for the people whose money they invest, their names and faces are not praised in the media and they are not held up as inspiring for doing such. The Wall Street banker is the perfect example of people who manage for a living as opposed to people who lead for a living.

However, do not be confused into thinking that management does not serve a valuable role in organizations. As the saying goes, "the devil is in the details" and so, it is necessary to have people who are able to make sure everything is in order. This is why lawyers, accountants, human resources personnel, quality control experts, financiers and the like are a part of corporate management teams. It is the role of the leader to be sure that the actions of these functionaries are in alignment with the mission and vision. The leader must also be a manager.

Another differentiating factor that separates most managers from leaders is from where the thinking originates. Managers tend to look at an objective in terms of what needs to be done then working to figure out how to do it. Leaders conversely approach things from an opposing perspective. Because they are visionaries by nature, the vision becomes *why* something is to be done. Then it must be worked out how to do it. This is explained in more detail in Chapter 5 when Simon Sinek's concept of the Golden Circle is discussed.

Why is it important to talk about inspirational leadership?

As Generation Y or Millenials take hold of more and more of the work force and as globalization continues to reshape and redefine the way business is done, the necessity for inspirational leadership becomes increasingly clear. People in this generational group born between the early 1980s and the early 2000s have a desire to do something meaningful with their efforts. They grew up learning about the way their parents and grandparents worked in factories, mines, building things and overall doing a lot of work they didn't feel personally connected with. For many it was a way to earn a living and get by. This is not what Millenials want.

This happens in a number of fields. There was an article published by the New South Wales Nursing Association that spoke about this very topic, explaining that employees will follow a good leader. It went on to explain that people look for a leader which inspires them and shows respect and value for what the employee bring to the organization. This isn't just the case in localized organizations either.

The desire and effectiveness of inspirational leadership is also a great tool in geographically dispersed teams. If you have a group based out of New York with offices in Chicago, Los Angeles, Hong Kong, Seoul, Singapore, London, Paris, Berlin and Moscow then you cannot oversee people's actions nearly as much as if you are a construction foreman on a work site. To do this effectively, a group of three professors who wrote on this subject, each working at different Universities and not closely located to one another, posed that the culture cannot be based on developing personal relationships as much as in more localized settings. Instead, socialized relationships based around a guiding set of ideas and principles are what are needed. Moreover, removing the emphasis on trust in management, and instead placing an emphasis on trust in team members is also necessary.

By basing the nature of the relationship around the vision, mission, and values of the organization, it becomes easier if people in those dispersed teams were to meet together because there would be established commonalities among everyone. With more distance among individuals, the need to have a strong connection to the core tenets of what the organization exists to do and how it goes about achieving it is crucial. Without a leader being able to model *ideal* behavior in front of other employees or go for that happy hour drink to chat it up a bit leaves less room for the leader to display ethics.

RQ What is your personal mission statement? (Your objectives and goals as an individual)

RQ What is the mission statement for the group you lead?

RQ What is the mission statement of the organization you work for?

RQ What do you consider your top 5 core values?
1.

2.

3.

4.

5.

RQ Now rank your core values.
2.
3.
4.
5.
5.

RQ Now try to define each of these values as you see them? As you come up with a definition try to dig deeper and ask *why* to arrive at a deeper understanding of what these values mean to you.

1.

2.

3.

4.

5.

RQ How does your own personal mission statement align with that of the group you lead and the organization as a whole?

RQ How do your personal core values align with those of the group you lead and the organization?

RQ Has any misalignment among these caused any problems?

Inspiration vs. motivation: how inspiration picks up when motivation reaches its limit

With inspiration already being a tricky word to pin down into a simple definition, it can be even more difficult to distinguish inspiration from motivation. People recognize that the two are different by using each word differently. Mother Teresa is considered an inspirational person by how she led her life in the service of others. The lottery motivates people to buy tickets especially when the prize gets higher and higher. Those who buy lottery tickets are motivated by a simple "If I do this, I might get that" mindset. This is different from a person who sees a place ravaged by war, poverty or a disaster, and decides to help build a school, donate money or commit themselves in any other way to help those afflicted.

Motivation tends to be guided by something benefiting the individual that is motivated. Winning the lottery will benefit you! Working harder to get a promotion at work benefits you! Being motivated to go work out after watching Rocky benefits you!

Inspiration on the other hand is something that typically hits an emotional nerve and causes the individual to do something for a higher cause, to help others, to create good in an area not their own or to crack a mystery so that others can have the knowledge. These differences are easily seen when compared to one another. When the hurricane hit the already impoverished country of Haiti in 2010, people flocked to send money and even travel to Haiti to help with cleanup and rebuilding. Most of the people who did this do not live in Haiti, are not from Haiti, and do not have close ties with the country, yet realize there is a great need to help a people deeply in need of assistance. The same happens whether it is Hurricane Katrina in 2005, the earthquake and following tsunami that hit Japan in 2011 or the tragic shooting that struck the small town community of Newtown, Connecticut in 2012.

This distinguishing factor, this key difference between the very nature of motivation and inspiration, is the sole reason why inspiration as a method of leadership is so much more powerful than simply being a motivator. People who are motivational speakers sell themselves short by only trying to be motivating. There is so much left on the table when a leader is only aiming to motivate those around them. Inspiration touches emotions, it becomes deeply personal, it brings individuals together under a common cause and one that is greater than themselves. When a leader aims to motivate they are using carrots and sticks, they are trying to push and prod, to coerce and this requires constant re-applying of motivational techniques, techniques in which their effectiveness wears off as time goes on unless the intensity grows greater and greater.

Robert Kiyosaki wrote about the pitfalls of motivation in his book "Rich Dad, Poor Dad." In it, he describes the rat race where people get a job because it pays well even though they don't particularly like the work they will be doing. After some time the worker then wants more money, not because they feel they are that much better at what they do or have improved their knowledge or skill level much more, but because money is the key motivator to their showing up for work every day to do the same activities day in and day out.

This leads to an uninspiring life and a worker who will not be a great contributor to the company.

Warren Buffett when describing his job as the Chief Executive Officer of Berkshire Hathaway, said that his main job was finding ways to keep the 15 or 20 managers who work with him excited and wanting to wake up to go to work at six o'clock in the morning since every one of them are wealthy beyond a need for more money. Each one could retire and not have to worry for the rest of their lives about money. This is a clear signal that Warren Buffett is an inspirational leader and not one who wishes to simply motivate his people. When they already make a lot of money and have accumulated a great deal of personal wealth, the idea of working for the paycheck is no longer what brings them to work.

The main office of Berkshire Hathaway is not in a lofty New York high rise overlooking any breath taking scenes, nor are they based in any other major metropolitan city that people may desire to work. Rather his company is based in Omaha, Nebraska. By the people who work directly under Buffett having more than enough wealth than they need means that the result is a group of people who want to work in the business and with the people they do because they wake up charged for what they do. The work turns them on and so do the people they interact with. This means that Buffett cannot get away with simply offering a pay or benefits increase for an unhappy employee because these are not the deciding factors as is the case with an overwhelming majority of employees. He must offer something even more. This also means that the employees want to be at work, they want to do what they do, again, not primarily for personal gain, but because they are inspired.

RQ Would you consider your current leadership style to be more motivational or inspirational?

RQ Are there certain functions or situations you find motivational techniques work better than trying to be inspirational? What are they?

RQ Can you think of any opportunities currently where you could move from motivation and toward inspiration?

From inspiration to action: the role of leadership

Inspiration is a terrible thing to waste! If you have been inspired yourself for whatever reason the question in mind should be, "Then what?" Inspiration is a complete waste if no action is taken. This is part of why citizens become frustrated when their leadership cannot agree on how to handle important issues such as the federal budget, abortion, gun control, prison reform, immigration, the quality of education or any other important issue.

Inspiration is also big business. John Bersin, a corporate leadership development expert, says that leadership development and supervisory/management training accounts for 21% of the training budget in corporate America even though management represents a small fraction of the total workforce. The reason for this is pretty simple when you think about it. Individual workers mainly influence only themselves. Managers influence groups of people. Therefore, if you have better managers then you can have happier more productive employees.

Some of the best inspirational leaders are the ones who took action for themselves without trying to directly influence others to take action. Later others will notice and figure it out and ask how they can be involved if there is a shared cause or vision. This is where people such as Martin Luther King Jr. have been able to have such large impact. Some however, choose to be more direct and intent on building power and trying to influence others.

Hitler was able to convince people to buy into the National Socialist party; that there was a superior race that deserved to rule the world and that it was necessary to conquer foreign lands and kill as many Jewish people as possible in the process. There was a defined vision that he was able to share with the hearts and minds of others causing them to take his vision as their own. He created inspiration and then led it in a specific direction.

John F. Kennedy. managed to create NASA and inspire the work that would put the first man on the moon in 1969. Martin Luther King Jr. preached non-violence by example and taught others how to protest and fight for civil rights. Jesus, through his teaching and way of living, inspired the creation of a whole new religion, Christianity, which would become one of the largest religions in the world by number of followers.

Inspiration is a powerful tool because of its emotional connection. Emotions are controlled in the Limbic system of the brain, the same portion that controls the survival instincts known as the 4 Fs: feeding, fighting, fleeing and fucking. Because of this emotional connection, inspiration can touch people very personally. For example, the horrific massacre at Sandy Hook elementary on December 14, 2012 sparked inspiration to make meaningful changes to how topics like mental health, guns and public safety are addressed in order to prevent further acts of terror. Events like these are deeply personal for many people because they are parents of small children, teachers, brothers, sisters or just reasonable people who recognize this senseless act was a tragedy and that something should be done.

The inspiration to make changes in hopes of preventing other acts of violence such as these grows stronger after similar events have happened at Columbine, Virginia Tech, the assassination attempt on Congresswoman Gabby Giffords in Arizona, the mass shooting at the Century Movie theatre in Aurora, Colorado, and at the shooting at the Clackamass Town Center in Portland Oregon. Individually an incident can be viewed as a one off and its reason for happening can be blamed on a culture of violence or mental illness and nothing significant is done. When there is a growing number of incidents on the other hand, people begin to recognize that something needs to change and begin to demand action from their leaders.

In times like these we look to our leaders to propose a plan of action. After all, this is why we picked them to be our leaders. When the terrorist attacks of September 11, 2001 happened, citizens were outraged, scared, saddened and heartbroken. However, the citizens had a feeling that something needed to be done. This was the first attack on American soil since the Japanese attack on Pearl Harbor December 7th, 1941. The day after Pearl Harbor President Franklin D. Roosevelt announced in his famous speech that included the line, "a day that will live in infamy," we were entering the war which had already been going on but the U.S. was not officially taking part. Two months after the attacks of 9/11 the U.S. military was launching Operation Enduring Freedom (O.E.F.) into Afghanistan where many of the members of the terrorist group Al-Qaeda were trained. The United States had not been involved in a conflict since Desert Storm in 1991 which was a short lived 100 hour ground assault decisively won by U.S. and coalition forces. Before that, nothing significant since the Vietnam War had happened militarily which had ended for the U.S.in 1973.

Some may argue that the inspiration aspect of leadership is only contained in the formulating of a vision and communicating that vision to others within the organization. Furthermore, some argue that it is then the role of management or motivation to convert the inspiration into action. When observed closely it can be seen that there is a mixture of the two.

Management is the organization of how the specific actions will take place. It includes tasks like timelines, defined objectives, and the roles that certain individuals will play and so on. Leadership is still required to ensure these things happen in a smooth and positive way. Though the two are separate, management and leadership are akin to a yin yang in that there is a little piece of one contained in its counterpart.

It is necessary for leaders to understand what skills they need to effectively lead, how to adapt their style to different cultures, personalities and situations. At times a leader may be trying to inspire his or her followers to change the fundamentals of the pre-established culture which may be tremendously difficult and require skillful play between the leader and followers. Inspirational leadership is a bit of a high stakes game because if all goes well you are the hero. If it fails then people lose faith and will not place much stock in further inspirational initiatives.

RQ What have been your experiences with trying to take a vision and convert it to action?

RQ What could you have done to improve the execution of your vision?

RQ What strategies or tactics did you use in executing your vision?

RQ Were your methods more grounded in motivation or inspiration?

RQ What lessons can you take from others who successfully took a vision into action and apply to your own scenario?

2. What inspiration looks like and where it comes from

Although it is difficult to find a definitive answer to the question, "what exactly is inspiration," it is much easier for people to give examples of people or events that have inspired them. Presented in this chapter is a short list of eight examples of people who are widely considered iconic and inspirational individuals as well as two examples that are not derived from people. Each person comes from a different background and inspired others in an arena separate from all others on the list making each example unique so as to show that inspiration is a universal quality that is not tethered only to certain places in society.

Inspiration is a powerful force being responsible for such historic events as the rise of the major religions of the world, empires, kings and queens, invention, scientific discovery, innovation and so much more. Questions that come to mind when contemplating the nature of inspiration are, "where does inspiration come from?"; and "how does inspiration happen?" We know that inspiration does not *just* happen; there is a catalyst that sets it in motion.

One thing most people would agree with however is that inspiration *does* happen. It is just a matter of *how?* It is easiest to put that which inspires us into three broad categories: 1) something that was meant to inspire 2) something not meant to inspire 3) inspiration from nature.

RQ Who or what inspires you?

RQ What is it about the person or thing that inspires you?

Example #1 (Military) Sergeant First Class Leroy Petry

The military has long been a rich source of inspiring individuals. A part of this is that it is seen as honorable and heroic to fight for a cause such as the protection of one's country. Furthermore, it has been a rich source of inspiring people because often times these people are put in difficult situations where their success in fighting through the immense challenges of combat and leading others to victory is an inspiring feat. Think of the landing on Omaha Beach in the invasion of Normandy, or the battle of Iwo Jima.

Sergeant First Class Leroy Petry undoubtedly was not aiming to inspire other people while performing on the mission that would later cause him to be awarded the Congressional Medal of Honor, the highest possible award given to a person in the United States military. There was never a thought of "Wow, think about how many people will be proud of me," or "I'm going to get the Medal of Honor for this." These thoughts would be the last thing a person such as Leroy Petry would consider. Below is an excerpt from President Barack Obama's remarks while awarding Petry the Congressional Medal of Honor at the White House on July 12, 2011.

"I want to take you back to the circumstances that led to this day. It's May 26, 2008, in the remote east of Afghanistan, near the mountainous border of Pakistan. Helicopters carrying dozens of elite Army Rangers race over the rugged landscape. And their target is an insurgent compound. The mission is high risk. It's broad daylight. The insurgents are heavily armed. But it's considered a risk worth taking because intelligence indicates that a top al Qaeda commander is in that compound.

Soon, the helicopters touch down, and our Rangers immediately come under fire. Within minutes, Leroy - then a Staff Sergeant - and another soldier are pushing ahead into a courtyard, surrounded by high mud walls. And that's when the enemy opens up with their AK-47s. Leroy is hit in both legs. He's bleeding badly, but he summons the strength to lead the other Ranger to cover, behind a chicken coop. He radios for support. He hurls a grenade at the enemy, giving cover to a third Ranger who rushes to their aid. An enemy grenade explodes nearby, wounding Leroy's two comrades. And then a second grenade lands - this time, only a few feet away.

Every human impulse would tell someone to turn away. Every soldier is trained to seek cover. That's what Sergeant Leroy Petry could have done. Instead, this wounded Ranger, this 28-year-old man with his whole life ahead of him, this husband and father of four, did something extraordinary. He lunged forward, toward the live grenade. He picked it up. He cocked his arm to throw it back.

What compels such courage? What leads a person to risk everything so that others might live? For answers, we don't need to look far. The roots of Leroy's valor are all around us.

We see it in the sense of duty instilled by his family, who joins us today - his father Larry, his mother Lorella, and his four brothers. Growing up, the walls of their home were hung with pictures of grandfathers and uncles in uniform, leading a young Leroy to believe "that's my calling, too."

We see it in the compassion of a high school student who overcame his own struggles to mentor younger kids to give them a chance. We see it in the loyalty of an Army Ranger who lives by a creed: "Never shall I fail my comrades." Or as Leroy puts it, "These are my brothers - family just like my wife and kids - and you protect the ones you love." And that's what he did that day when he picked up that grenade and threw it back - just as it exploded.

With that selfless act, Leroy saved his two Ranger brothers, and they are with us today. His valor came with a price. The force of the blast took Leroy's right hand. Shrapnel riddled his body. Said one of his teammates, "I had never seen someone hurt so bad." So even his fellow Rangers were amazed at what Leroy did next. Despite his grievous wounds, he remained calm. He actually put on his own tourniquet. And he continued to lead, directing his team, giving orders - even telling the medics how to treat his wounds.

When the fight was won, as he lay in a stretcher being loaded onto a helicopter, one of his teammates came up to shake the hand that Leroy had left. "That was the first time I shook the hand of someone who I consider to be a true American hero," that Ranger said. Leroy Petry "showed that true heroes still exist and that they're closer than you think."

That Ranger is right. Our heroes are all around us. They're the millions of Americans in uniform who have served these past 10 years, many —— like Leroy —— deploying tour after tour, year after year. On the morning of 9/11, Leroy was training to be a Ranger, and as his instructor got the terrible news, they told Leroy and his class, "Keep training, you might be going to war." Within months Leroy was in Afghanistan for the first of seven deployments since 9/11."

-President Barack Obama

The idea that a person after being injured in both legs, being pinned under gunfire and grenade, could apply his own tourniquet after having his hand blown off by an enemy grenade when trying to throw it back and still continuing to fight and lead those around him is in no doubt inspirational. This example perfectly illustrates the power of the human spirit, the abilities of the human body, and that under the most intense circumstances a person can overcome the difficulties that lie ahead. Leroy Petry is in every sense of the word an American hero. He did not consider himself a hero, was not thinking of medals or awards, but was only thinking to take care of his fellow Rangers and not give up.

Sergeant First Class Petry is part of the elite light infantry regiment of the U.S. Army called the Rangers. Rangers endure intensive training and most of the people who report to Ranger school do not graduate. These soldiers are given very little to eat during their training, very little sleep and very little room for error. The rigors of this training program that soldiers voluntarily put themselves into has a distinct and important purpose: to train the mind first, the body second.

Army Rangers are a part of the Special Operations component of the Army. They are assigned to high risk missions like the one SFC Petry was sent on. These men must be able to trust each person on their team. Each Ranger realizes that although they are highly trained and skilled individuals they are all still a part of a team. There is a camaraderie that is built through hardship such as combat. It is the strength of character developed through training and experience that allows people like Leroy Petry to be an inspiring figure.

Example #2 (Civil Rights) Dr. Martin Luther King Jr.

Dr. Martin Luther King Jr. is an incredible example of someone who has been no doubt inspirational. Growing up in the deep south of Georgia, King would witness and himself fall victim to the harsh brutality that was reality for many African Americans in the Jim Crow era. The routine beatings, lynchings, and public acts of humiliation that were used in an effort to make African Americans feel as though they were second class citizens did not deter King. He saw that African Americans were freed by law for nearly one hundred years but were still not truly free in action.

King's commitment to nonviolent civil disobedience was essential to the successes that his movement would achieve. Clearly inspired by the example and philosophy of Mohandas Gandhi, King realized that if he was to result to violence that it would only serve to give those who wished to continue the oppression an excuse. He understood that as Gandhi said, "An eye for an eye leaves the whole world blind."

Undoubtedly his methods required great courage; knowing that many would be beaten, jailed and killed for their activism. This fact must have weighed heavily on King. Martin Luther King knew that if the injustices were made public and that if African Americans could stand together peacefully that it made the case for equality that much stronger. As an educated minister King was able to use the fact that America was founded as a nation based on Christian principles to his advantage. Urging people to not fall into the trap of violence, rather to struggle on peacefully as did Jesus, that it would put the civil rights movement on the moral high ground.

King had a number of great accomplishments throughout his short lived 39 year life. For an African American living in the South, the idea of receiving a college education was not a reality for most. He would not only attend college, but he also went on to receive a Ph.D. in Systematic Theology from Boston University at the age of 26 in 1955. That was not all he would achieve.

It was also in 1955 when a young Martin Luther King Jr. would lead the Montgomery Bus Boycott. The boycott lasted 385 days eventually resulting in a United States District Court ruling that ended racial segregation on all Montgomery public buses.

In 1963, Dr. King's efforts along with those of other civil rights and labor groups led to the March on Washington where he would give his famous "I Have A Dream" speech. In the speech, King urged African Americans to continue to work toward civil rights and justice under the law. He also plead to African Americans to not fall into the trap of violence that some other groups were turning to, most notably the Black Panthers and the ideas that Malcolm X promoted. In addition, Dr. King made a point of mentioning that not all white people were against the idea of equality, even pointing out that several were in attendance on the day of his famous speech.

"We must forever conduct our struggle on the high plane of dignity and discipline. We must not allow our creative protest to degenerate into physical violence....As we walk, we must make the pledge that we shall always march ahead. We cannot turn back...I am not unmindful that some of you have come here out of great trials and tribulations. Some of you have come fresh from narrow jail cells. Some of you have come from areas where your quest for freedom left you battered by the storms of persecution and staggered by the winds of police brutality. You have been the veterans of creative suffering. Continue to work with the faith that unearned suffering is redemptive."

-Martin Luther King Jr., I Have a Dream Speech, August 28, 1963

Author Simon Sinek contends in his Tedx talk that the difference between King and others throughout history who do not achieve such success is that King did not seek fame, but in having a vision that other people took as their own. He further argues that this is why King did not give the "I have a plan speech". Sinek notes that people are not inspired by politicians who give multipoint plans yet are inspired by those who have a unifying vision.

The following year in 1964 Dr. King would receive the Nobel Peace Prize. In 1977 he posthumously received the Presidential Medal of Freedom, in 1986 Martin Luther King Jr. day was established as a U.S. federal holiday. And in 2004, the Congressional Gold Medal was posthumously awarded to Dr. King.

King's most important achievements in the struggle for justice and equality were the Civil Rights Act of 1964 and the Voting Rights Act of 1965. Sadly King was assassinated in 1968 just a few short years after the passage of these bills. King's example serves not only for African Americans or even those living in America for that matter, but for people living all over the world. The courage that Dr. King demonstrated so powerfully throughout his life by standing for a cause he felt deeply passionate about can be seen today.

A wonderful example of this is Malala Yousafzai. This young brave girl lives in Pakistan; a country known for its repressive practices with regard to educating girls. Young Malala who speaks English very well and loves to learn spoke out against the Taliban who began having influence in her native Swat valley. Starting at the young age of only eleven and a half, Malala began writing a blog for the BBC under a pseudonym chronicling her experience living under the repressiveness of the Taliban.

On the day of October 9, 2012 while riding the bus home from school, Yousafzai was attacked by a masked gunman. After threatening to shoot everyone on the bus if she was not identified, the gunman shot Malala directly in the head, sending the bullet through her head, neck and ending in her shoulder. Fortunately she survived the vicious attack and recovered. She continues to speak out against the Taliban and has become an inspiring figure for her struggle for not only freedom and justice, but also for every child's ability to have access to basic education.

Example #3 (Business) Steve Jobs

Steve Jobs, the eponymous co-founder of Apple Computers, is the pure embodiment of the inspirational business leader. Jobs shares the same qualities that are inextricably bound to all of the best examples of inspirational leadership regardless of where in society they are to be found.

Jobs was at the tip of the spear for what would be the burgeoning personal computers industry that would see rapid growth throughout the 1980s and 1990s. To understand how someone like a Steve Jobs exists requires understanding that he was more of a visionary who could see something that was possible and then set out to create what was in his mind.

He was notorious for being a perfectionist when it came down to every last detail of the software and to the design and construction of hardware. This would cause multiple projects throughout his time to be pushed back sometimes teetering on the point of the product being obsolete by the time it would be released because so much attention was paid to the details. Such was the case with the NeXT Cube which would prove to be a disappointment in the market once released.

Steve was an individual who like many were not always so sure of what would happen. In the very beginning it wasn't clear whether or not Apple would become the powerhouse company it is known as today. Jobs faced many challenges during his life including the complicated relationship with his daughter Lisa to his being ousted from Apple in 1985.

After leaving Apple, Jobs created NeXT to compete with Apple which in its eleven years of existence had sold only about 50,000 computers. The strategy for NeXT was to focus on higher education and business sales. This strategy did not prove to be as successful as was hoped. People were seduced by the idea however; Ross Perot invested some $20 million dollars in the company and Canon initially invested $100 million and another $30 million later on.

On the side, Steve had purchased Pixar for $10 million and after sinking millions of his own money he tried to sell the company many times over after a lack of any successful venture besides some animated commercials that did not cover the immense cost being poured into the company.

Steve Jobs however continued to move forward even when the situation did not appear to look so bright. In 1995, Pixar, in partnership with Disney, would release *Toy Story*, a movie that would change the course for Pixar. Pixar would go on to do several more successful films with Disney to include *A Bug's Life* and *Finding Nemo.*

While Steve Jobs was trying to balance the challenges of NeXT and Pixar in the early and mid 1990s, his former company Apple was not faring too well either. Jobs was needed as sales had slumped and needed an infusion of the special sauce that he provided in the early days that brought Apple on to the scene. In 1996 Apple purchased NeXT and brought Steve back where he would lead the company until his retirement in 2005 due to his battle with pancreatic cancer.

Jobs simplified the product line and provided a sense of focus to the efforts of those working in the company. He was personally involved in pretty much every aspect from deciding which products to focus on to talking with those working on projects to get a sense of their worth to the company and to the market, to being involved with software and product design.

Among the innovations of Steve Jobs, perhaps the one he is best known for is the ability to create a beautifully designed product that was technologically superior to everything else that was available that also maintained a focus on improving people's lives. It was Jobs who understood that the movement of the computer and electronics market was toward a digital lifestyle in the early 2000s. This notion that many other people in the business did not hold is what led him to pursue products such as the iPod, iTunes, iPhone and iPad.

Realizing that one of the challenges of making and trying to sell such fundamentally different products would be in people's ability to understand how they worked. Most people are used to the Microsoft operating system that is found on most computers since the Apple operating system is only found on Apple computers. It was for this reason that Apple created retail stores where people were able to take these products for a test drive. The stores were staffed with people that could answer questions and explain how the devices worked and how the customer would benefit from using the product. The retail stores proved to be successful beyond expectation in moving products and have been the site of many long lines whenever new Apple products are released.

In the end Steve Jobs proved to be somewhat of a phoenix. A person who experienced success followed by a sort of death with his ouster at Apple then his second rising that started in 1996 as he returned to Apple once again. His ideas were often well ahead of their time and what everyone else was doing causing some to not get on board because they were so far ahead. Jobs found a way to still create the amazing products he envisioned while explaining them to his customers in a way they could understand and fall in love with.

Example #4 (Politician) Theodore Roosevelt

President Theodore Roosevelt led an extraordinary life and was in every sense of the phrase triumphantly American. He is routinely included in a list of top Presidents in U.S. History along with the likes of George Washington, Abraham Lincoln and Franklin Delano Roosevelt.

There are those whose lives inspire us because they are examples of someone overcoming personal challenges, willing to challenge conventional wisdom, and unwilling to accept something on the basis that it is simple. This is exactly what Teddy Roosevelt embodied. As a child he dealt with asthma, struggling with weakened lungs his father at times would have to carry him at night to comfort him. As a child he was small and physically weak. His father served as a motivating force in his life. At his father's suggestion Roosevelt began exercising regularly and even took boxing lessons.

His family was wealthy and well connected which Roosevelt used as a tool to maximize his potential. T.R. as he was sometimes known, did not rest on this fact; he did not want to take jobs out of ease nor did he want to do the bare minimum or accept bribes as would have been easy. Rather he chose to do the exact opposite.

During his time as the New York City police commissioner, Roosevelt would patrol at night catching police officers while on duty in bars and telling them to get back out on the streets. He would observe crimes and took action to make changes to a long broken police force.

Roosevelt resigned as Assistant Secretary of the Navy at the outbreak of the Spanish American war. He helped form a band of volunteer ranchers and cowboys forming a regiment known as the Rough Riders. Roosevelt himself started as a Lieutenant Colonel and was later promoted to Colonel, serving as Commander of the Regiment. Roosevelt and his Rough Riders would take the charge at San Juan in the Spanish American war. Roosevelt himself was even recommended for the Congressional Medal of Honor and was awarded the Nobel Peace Prize for his part in brokering an end to he Russo-Japanese War.

He took risks. He left New York to move to the badlands of North Dakota to take up cattle ranching. He was not raised as a cowboy or as a pioneer man but that did not stop or deter Roosevelt. It was difficult and many cowboys could tell he was not in his element but his work ethic and commitment earned him respect on the plains of North Dakota. During a Presidential campaign event in 1912, Roosevelt was shot in the chest yet went on to deliver his speech with the bullet still in his chest. He remarked, "You see, it takes more than one bullet to kill a bull moose".

Signs of Teddy's wealth were apparent during his activities. His uniforms while serving in the Army were tailor made to his measurements and the knife he used while cattle ranching on the plains was purchased from Tiffany and Company. These did not define T.R. They just added to his character.

He later would become one the most influential leaders in American history. A great amount of his personal drive came from the challenges of his childhood. Throughout the rest of his entire life he was always willing to challenge the status quo; he did not believe that because something was the established norm that it could not be changed. He saw people who lacked the personal character and conviction to do what he felt was the right thing to do. Theodore Roosevelt was a staunch advocate for a strong moral character and held the belief that people deserved to be dealt fairly.

In 1910 while in Paris, France, Roosevelt gave a speech titled "Citizenship in a Republic" which included the following famous lines:

"It is not the critic who counts: not the man who points out how the strong man stumbles or where the doer of deeds could have done better. The credit belongs to the man who is actually in the arena, whose face is marred by dust and sweat and blood, who strives valiantly, who errs and comes up short again and again, because there is no effort without error or shortcoming, but who knows the great enthusiasms, the great devotions, who spends himself for a worthy cause; who, at the best, knows, in the end, the triumph of high achievement, and who, at the worst, if he fails, at least he fails while daring greatly, so that his place shall never be with those cold and timid souls who knew neither victory nor defeat."

-President Theodore Roosevelt, 1910

This quote is a perfect explanation of the attitude that Teddy Roosevelt carried with him. He was strong willed and unintimidated having believed in the West African proverb "Speak softly and carry a big stick; you will go far." Roosevelt was also forward thinking about conservation having created the National Park system. He was in favor of equal rights for women and advocated for people being practical while still aiming high.

Example #5 Religion

It is not fair to choose only one religion or one religious leader in large part because the whole of the establishment as it is known is inspired by the idea of a God or Gods. God is referred to as the idea of God only because it is not the intent of this writing to take a stance one way or another about God or religion.

Regardless of whether you hold a personal belief in the existence of God or a supreme being or not, it cannot be argued that religion and a belief in God has made a significant influence on the history and culture of human civilization. The idea that every person can have a personal relationship with a divine being that is responsible for everything we experience in life is quite incredible. The common thread among religions which compels people to lead a moral life is that they will be either rewarded in the afterlife or punished for living immorally.

Religion as a social entity serves to make an attempt at providing answers to many of the questions people commonly ask such as "why we are here on Earth?", or "how were things created?" There is an overriding sense of moral authority found within the various religious establishments based on the word of God. Organized religions also create a social bond where people are able to hold similar views and share a strength in numbers mentality by being unified under a common belief system. This is also seen in political movements, social causes, and national cultures in large part because as humans we are social and group oriented by nature, seeking to gain acceptance of our peers.

Arts and culture are areas that have been clearly influenced by religion. For example, some of the most beautiful music has been inspired by the idea of God, like Handel's The Messiah. Or consider the Sistine Chapel ceiling which was painted by Michelangelo and is considered a masterpiece. Religious symbols are also found in elements of government and politics on everything from money to buildings and even laws based on the moral teachings of a given religion.

The will of God or the teachings of God have inspired people to perform amazing things throughout the ages and even today via their charitable activities. Some of these positive activities include feeding the poor, couple's counseling, addiction treatment and providing medical services to those in need.

Religious interpretations have also compelled many to commit unfortunate acts of violence and obscenity at just about any point in history that religion has been in existence. Two simple examples would be the sexual abuses that have been uncovered in the Catholic church and the modern day Jihad or Holy War being waged by a group within the Muslim community against western nations, primarily western Europe and the United States.

Religion as a component of human society is able to teach the lesson quite clearly that inspiration is a double edged sword, capable of achieving amazing humanitarian results or serving tremendous harm and destruction. This is not to say that the other examples of this list do no carry their own negative attributes. This is to say however, that ethics is an integral part of any serious leadership discussion.

Example #6 (Media) Oprah Winfrey

Oprah Winfrey it goes without need to mention, is a significant force in the American media landscape. Her influence stretches far and wide surpassing what most onlookers would have considered even vaguely possible given the circumstances in which Oprah has as her background. It is these very circumstances combined with decisions contrary to conventional wisdom of the time that would later prove to be the root of her success.

Oprah is a source of inspiration for women the world over as to what it means to be a strong and independent person coming from modest means. She stood as an example of what a person is capable of achieving given enough hard work and sincerity to one's own beliefs. So what is it that makes Oprah so damn influential?

After all, there are many other people who have hosted talk shows before including: Phil Donahue, Jerry Springer, Geraldo Rivera, Jay Leno, Jimmy Kimmel, Jimmy Fallon, Craig Kilborn, David Letterman, George Lopez, Conan O'Brian, Dennis Miller, Stephen Colbert, Jon Stewart, and Montel Williams. But wait those are all men.

What about other female talk show hosts? Yes there are a few like: Ricki Lake, Sally Jesse Rafael, Tyra Banks, Ellen DeGeneres, Joy Behar, Katie Couric, Rosie O'Donnell, Sara Gilbert, Whoopi Goldberg, Chelsea Handler, Star Jones, Lisa Ling, Joan Lunden, Sharon Osbourne, Jane Pauley, Kelly Ripa, Joan Rivers, Dr. Ruth Westheimer, Wendy Williams, Meredith Viera and Laura Schlessinger.

Clearly it is not that she is female or African American or even the combination of the two. No, it is more than that. Her reputation is one of sincerity, openness and a deep sense of humanity. She has spoken publicly on her nationally syndicated talk show about her experiences of childhood abuse and growing up wearing dresses made of potato sacks because there was not enough money to buy her a dress.

Similar to the story of Teddy Roosevelt, the hardships that Oprah faced and chose to overcome with hard work and determination are foundational to the future successes she would enjoy later throughout her life. She found a way to not only bring important issues to the forefront of the conversation, but through her honesty both with the audience and everyone watching at home, was able to make the conversation substantive and penetrating. As television shows in the 1990s were becoming filled more and more with so called "tabloid topics", Winfrey resisted. This would prove to be a smart move helping to build her loyal base even larger.

By staying true to herself in the belief of making an emotional connection with the audience she was able to take the last place show *AM Radio* and within months over take the then dominant Phil Donahue putting her show in first place. Later she would syndicate her show as *The Oprah Winfrey Show* and enjoy a run of 25 years until bringing the show to an end, not because the show lost viewership or was failing, but to pursue other ventures in life.

She is also credited with bringing elements of her personal life and beliefs into the themes of the show such as literature, self improvement and spirituality. For example, with her book club she was able to feature a title and have it almost guaranteed to be an instant bestseller. She brought important issues deeply ingrained in American culture to the forefront of the conversation when other shows avoided such topics or did so in a way that did not connect with people.

As if having her own nationally syndicated television show that maintained a strong base of support wasn't enough, Oprah would also create her own television network OWN and the magazine *O*. She even threw her support behind Barack Obama in both the 2008 and 2012 Presidential elections. Winfrey did maintain a consistent practice of not allowing politicians while running for office to come on to her show to promote themselves rather choosing to allow them to be a guest after the election.

Oprah is also loved for her generosity. She has given brand new cars to complete audiences as well as Australian vacations. Ironically brands are working to bring a personal and individualized experience back to what they provide to customers after so many had chosen to switch to automated systems. Oprah has maintained this very human sense the entire time. When people see that you stay true to yourself when it is easy to go the other way it sends a message that you have a personal sense of integrity. Customers respect and appreciate that quality. As consuming becomes more social people align themselves with brands that share their own values and beliefs; the ones who come across as being full of people and not machines and recordings.

Example #7 Nature

Understanding our world both on Earth and in space is a task humans have set out on and are nowhere near completing. With land only accounting for about one third of Earth's surface, there is a great deal of underwater discovery that has yet to take place. Part of this is because we have yet to develop sufficient technology to explore the depths and most extreme areas of our oceans. We have only recently in terms of human existence figured out where all of the land is on Earth. Even knowing where the land is does not mean we have discovered everything there is on it. Continuously there are new species found that were never before known in the Amazon. This yearning for understanding, for being able to put all of the piece of the puzzle together so that one day we can have a complete picture of our planet is quite exhilarating.

Staring up at the heavens contemplating the many mysteries they contain has inspired many throughout history to try to understand how they got there, why they are the way they are, and how they matter to us. Human are by nature curious and want to know about that which is around us. There have been many explanations and theories about the cosmos, so much so that entire areas of Science are heavily influenced by them: Astronomy, Physics, Biology, Geology and son on.

It would be easy to simply profile an influential scientist like Isaac Newton, Albert Einstein or Neil DeGrasse Tyson whose contributions to science have no doubt inspired others. Each of these scientists and several more unmentioned scientists were not included because the source of their inspiration was a shared one. It was when they looked up at the immense beauty and mystery of the stars as they hung in the sky in wonderment and wanted to understand the how and why of such things.

Currently with all of the research and discovery of scientists it turns out that we as humans can only account for roughly four percent of the universe. Between dark energy and dark matter which make up about ninety-six percent of the universe this leaves a very small amount that includes all of the planets, stars, asteroids, meteors, and everything else we can see in the universe. Even with the latest in scientific discovery we only know that dark matter and dark energy exist because their effects on what is around them can be observed though we cannot answer any more than that about what it is nor its role in the universe as a whole.

Scientists are still working to develop a string theory. Essentially quantum mechanics which currently provides a workable set of laws explaining how things move and function on a subatomic level do not comply with law of general relativity that was summarized by Albert Einstein when he created his famous $E=mc^2$ equation when you bring the scale of things close together.

Another amazing question that still eludes scientists is why the universe is expanding at an accelerating rate. This observation is contrary to Newtonian physics that dictates that something in motion will slow due to friction unless there is a force greater than friction being exerted upon it. The Big Bang is estimated to have occurred over thirteen billion years ago. Why is it that the universe is still exploding outward in all directions and at an ever increasing rate? This takes scientists far into the theoretical realm with ideas of multiple universes or the possible effects of dark matter and dark energy.

The Great Pyramids are built in alignment with stars as are other manmade structures found on Earth's surface. There are paintings, sculptures, cave drawings, contraptions and many other attempts to recreate what is seen in the night sky. Each of these are examples of how nature inspired action. Nature never directed or dictated such things. It was a person who was inspired and conceptualized how to interpret that inspiration.

The very fact that we understand so little about so much of our surroundings provides a deep source of inspiration knowing there are thousands of discoveries just waiting to be figured out. Knowing how much previous discoveries have impacted life on Earth and wondering how many more of these big discoveries are left and which ones will happen in our lifetime is more than enough inspiration to keep legions of scientists feverishly working away on research.

Example #8 Global Threats

Threats are the other primary source of inspiration aside from those derived from people or from the understanding of what is around us. It becomes quite obvious that a part of this is because of the biological desire for self preservation that has helped keep humans and every other living creature adapting to survive throughout time. However, it is something more than that. Global threats are grand in scale and require great amounts of effort and resource to effectively tackle.

More recently we can see this same thought process take hold as we are confronted with threats. People band together behind a cause, donate money, time, resources and effort to improving or eliminating the threat. The 20th century saw the discovery of vaccinations for diphtheria (1923), tetanus and tuberculosis (1927), yellow fever (1953), measles (1963), mumps (1967), Rubella, (1969) and Pneumonia (1977).

Even with all these impressive achievements in less than one hundred years time there are still many more threats. Currently there is work being done to combat the onslaught of climate changes effects, food shortage, water shortage, and an increasing population. Just those four are grand in scale and will require cooperation and compromise from governments, non profits, business and private citizens. As if it were only these four that people had to concern themselves about it would be daunting enough, however those are only some of the most severe global threats in existence.

Land is a resource that cannot really be created. Therefore, people cannot build out so easily. Rather, they must build up. By not building up, precious land that is necessary for farming, ranching and forestry is removed therefore destabilizing the balance of resources to meet the demands humans place on those resources.

With an increasing population also comes more demand for water. Companies have found many creative ways to add ingredients to water to provide a better taste causing reduced consumption of water as is the case with soda, energy drinks, coffee and alcohol. Unfortunately, these ingredients often times provide poor amounts of nutrition and contribute to obesity and other health issues that confront society. Water is still an essential ingredient to life.

RQ Are there any qualities you found in the examples that you possess? What are they?

RQ Can you think of any ways to build up the qualities you find particularly inspiring in yourself?

3. The Science of Leadership

This chapter is not as focused on inspirational leadership as the other chapters in this book; instead, it takes a scientific look at leadership as a whole. This is because it is important to look at how inspirational leadership as a style or method of leadership fits into the whole picture of leadership. There are a number of lessons from the established body of scientific research that can be applied to the various facets of leadership such as group dynamics, change initiatives, social responsibility and so on.

Science is a great way to test hypotheses and give merit to claims once only standing on anecdotal or very subjective evidence. This turns out to be the case in leadership development training programs. These programs oftentimes rely on the subjective results of 360 degree surveys given to the leader his/herself, the ones who report to the leader, the leader's colleagues, and the person or people to which the leader reports. Recent scientific research has helped create an added level of accuracy to these programs.

The surveys management consulting firms use to gauge a leader may ask questions such as, "do you feel your supervisor empathizes with you?" or "on a scale of 1-10, do you feel your manager understands your needs?" This makes it far too easy for people who have a bad feeling toward their manager, possibly because they feel they were passed up for promotion, to inaccurately skew the results in a negative way. On the other hand, if someone is close friends with their manager, possibly because of some personal relationship extending outside of the workplace, it can skew the results in an inaccurately positive way. Hopefully these outlier effects are detected and taken into account but there still exists a high potential for inaccurate results.

Because of these problems, there are efforts to improve the metrics that can be applied to such an abstract concept such as leadership. It is far more comforting when there are measurable improvements in efficiency, productivity, processes, the implementation of new policies or procedures, cost savings, sales growth, or anything else that can be directly measured especially in terms of dollars.

This qualitative conundrum that exists in leadership may be a big reason companies prefer to use management consultants over leadership consultants and proof of this is evidenced in the fact that the term management consultant is much more commonplace in business than leadership consultant. Management is based on the principle of finding what can be measured and improved. This way of thinking gave rise to DMAIC (Define Measure Analyze Improve Control) that is a core principle of the Six Sigma process improvement method.

The desire for metrics and maximum output stands in the face of employee complaints in many companies that there is too much management, but never do you hear of employees complaining about too much leadership. Being able to have concrete numbers to go off of makes it easier for a company to justify making the investment into management consultants. If a company is going to invest the kind of money that consulting services can cost they want to have something to show for it and numbers are reassuring yet do not tell the whole picture.

Leadership is influenced by a number of social science fields including Sociology, Anthropology, Psychology and Communication. Each of these fields aid those who study leadership by providing a body of research that produce explanations for why and how certain behaviors occur, how people interact and communicate with one another in various contexts, the inner workings of power and group dynamics, how people handle stress, as well as how they learn skills and tasks. Every one of these contributions provides a tremendous benefit to the leader who can understand the research and determine which specific needs exist in an organization and how best to introduce and implement the lessons from these various disciplines in a positive and productive manner.

Thankfully science is coming to the rescue; primarily in the areas of Sociology, Psychology and Neuroscience. Sociology examines human social interaction which is a paramount topic in leadership. Psychology offers an area of study called Emotional Intelligence, pioneered by Daniel Goleman, to fill in some of the gaps of current leadership development programs. In neuroscience, research is being done in an effort to create a link between the attributes of inspirational leaders and brain activity in specific areas of the brain.

Sociology

Humans are very curious and social creatures. This curiosity has led to the study of a menagerie of subjects. One such topic of study is Sociology; or the study of human social behavior. As humans live in groups and most groups have a power structure, it is valuable to consider the study of human social behavior and what it teaches us about leadership.

Biologically we have a need for social activity. Solitary confinement used as a method of punishment in many prisons is a form of social deprivation in which a person is denied this basic human desire. Through behavior, humans try to meet certain biological and social needs i.e. friends, family, mates, and other social relationships. From these interactions and associations, people try to establish and reinforce a sense of belonging and social acceptance. Sociology studies the behavior by which we attempt to meet these needs and desires.

All organizations are comprised of groups and many groups are formed into teams. All teams are groups though not all groups are teams. It is from these social structures that it becomes necessary for leaders to understand the dynamics of both groups and teams. What is the difference and why does it matter?

Marvin Shaw defines a group as, "two or more persons who are interacting with one another in such a manner that each person influences and is influenced by each other" such as a book club. Conversely, according to Jon Katzenbach and Douglas Smith, a teams is "a unit of two or more people with complementary skills who are committed to a common purpose, set of performance goals and expectations, for which they hold themselves accountable" such as a sports team.

Because any organization at its core is a group of people, if you intend to lead that group toward achieving a goal, it would be wise to understand group dynamics as well as the principles of leadership that go along with both groups and teams. Not everything is perfect, there are both pros and cons of groups and teams.

Research shows that groups out perform individuals with a series of problem solving skills. Groups also encourage a collective conscious because they can share ideas and use collaborative learning to accomplish tasks. Groups also facilitate continuous improvement and innovation by having various perspectives from which to draw. There is also typically less pressure on individuals when members make equitable contributions. However, not everything is so great when dealing with a group or team.

A lack of efficient and clear direction can create coordination loss where efforts are not used to their fullest potential. Motivation loss can also occur as members become less engaged with the group's purpose or accomplishment. At times group members decide to leave the work of the group to the other members thereby engaging in what is known as social loafing. There are also times when the entire group begins to think the same way or are influenced to not challenge the authority's thoughts which leads to a concept known as groupthink.

A group can be anything from just a few people all the way up to the whole of humanity. People use context to distinguish how they align with a particular group at a particular time. For example, you can be proud to be American yet not proud about certain events in American history such as the Japanese internment or slavery. You can be proud to be American yet also recognize that we as humans must unite at certain times to confront global challenges.

Culture is an important aspect of social groups. One important facet of a culture is the group or society's ability to establish and regulate a set of accepted social behaviors. These accepted social behaviors help form the D.N.A. of a social group. Laws, courts, police, traditions, national holidays, patriotic songs, and so much more exist in part to define the culture of the group as a whole. Social pressure is often used to influence behavior in the absence of formal authority. Each serve as a way of defining and deterring what social behaviors that society in general has agreed are unacceptable such as murder, robbery, or the exploitation of others.

When a person arrives fresh to a social group they are unfamiliar with, they may experience culture shock. This culture shock is experienced when people change schools, travel to a new country, or start a new job. A process of socialization helps orient a newcomer to a social group by educating him or her on the norms of the group. This is the reason most companies have some form of company orientation for new employees. Zappos takes the idea of socialization a bit further and publishes an annual Culture Book composed of photos from events of the previous year and entries from employees about what the company means to them which is just one piece of well thought out and well executed program of employee engagement.

Failing to properly go through the socialization process with newcomers can prove to be damaging. It can lead to cliques being formed, inter-group aggression by different divisions within a company, or even favoritism and bias. Bob Nardelli was famously ousted as C.E.O. of Home Depot. He had received the job offer just 10 minutes after leaving Chrysler and thought he knew what needed to be done. He brought an autocratic leadership style while implementing Six Sigma principles which eroded the entrepreneurial spirit of many Home Depot employees. This freedom that employees had lost was a valued part of their association with Home Depot. This change led to reduced employee morale and eventually the ouster of Bob Nardelli. This is a great example of where relying too heavily on metrics and the maximization of output can actually result in a drop in productivity due to sapped employee morale and motivation.

Chrysler suffered after merging with Daimler-Benz AG in 1998. One of the biggest issues was of a culture clash in which Daimler believed that the people of Chrysler would simply assimilate into the Daimler way. Daimler and Chrysler are companies based in two separate countries with long and proud histories of automotive success. Each company has a different culture not only within the company, but nationally as well. From this example, it is easy to see that there was a failure to properly go through the socialization process between the two groups which could have created a different outcome altogether.

When Chrysler later merged with Fiat in 2009, a different approach was taken. Instead, Fiat decided to create a plan of equality in which people from Chrysler in the United States would travel to Italy where Fiat is based and vice versa. This has led to a much more successful transition between the two different companies, from two different countries, with two different languages, and who are each successful in making vehicles in two different segments. By properly going through the socialization process, a deeper level of group cohesion between the two companies was achieved.

Group cohesion refers to how well members work together and get along. Workplace tension is costly as it can take away from productivity, morale, require intervention by management, and can lead to increased absenteeism and turnover. For leaders it is worthwhile to understand how to build group cohesion as it can be a useful tool for keeping people together especially when challenging times occur.

It is good to get groups together for fun activities to allow for stress release and facilitate social bonding which can help strengthen working relationships. This can be as simple as planning a happy hour after work one Friday per month. Consider the demographics of the group, the intent of the event and what activities would be both appropriate and appreciated.

More structured team building activities are a great way to build problem solving skills in team settings. They serve as a way to intellectually stimulate people without having the typical work pressure. This can range from paintball to a friendly game of softball. Notice how team building activities have more defined member roles and goals in contrast to group activities where everyone is just getting together to do the same thing.

Although group cohesion is helpful, it is not required. An interesting fact is that research does not indicate cohesion equals group effectiveness. This is because when a group of people are high in cohesion they are at a risk of group think. Group think refers to when members do not challenge the group or leader's thinking or actions. Either everyone is going along and thinking the same way, or people are unwilling to speak up. This can lead to disastrous results as was the case with the J.F.K. led botched Bay of Pigs mission of 1961. It is still good practice to foster at lease some level of group cohesion.

If people feel as though they are part of a team where everyone contributes, then individuals are sometimes willing to put in more effort because of their identity and commitment with the group. The U.S. military is well known for having some of the highest amounts of cohesion. This is seen especially so in its elite special operations units such as the Army Rangers, Navy SEALs, Air Force Pararescuemen, and Marine Force Recon.

There was a matrix used in one of my leadership courses that looked at the willingness and ability of a person. This matrix connects with the concept of group satisfaction. Essentially, it showed that someone was in either one of four possible places on the matrix. They could be willing but not able; willing and unable; unwilling and unable; or willing and able. Ideally you want someone both willing and able.

If group members are dissatisfied however, they may drift from willing and able to unwilling and able. This negative dynamic can spread to other members causing the entire groups to lose desire to perform the task at hand. For this reason, it is valuable to conduct management surveys or employee engagement surveys. It is good practice to do these annually or if there has been a significant event that may impact satisfactions and/or performance. These tools are useful because it is important to members that thy have a mechanism by which they can vent problems and know that management will be aware.

Additionally, it is advisable to maintain a sense of the pulse between the balance of self and group identity. As social creatures, human beings belong to a variety of groups including: family, friends, work, community, political, sports, race, gender, sexual orientation, religion, national, and so on. It is because of the wide number of groups who we are members of that it is important to be a member while maintaining our sense of personal identity.

This quote by Friederich Nietzsche eloquently sums up the challenge of balancing self and group identity, "The individual has always had to struggle to keep from being overwhelmed by the tribe. If you try it you will be lonely often, and sometimes frightened. But no price is too high for the privilege of owning yourself." Nietzsche paints a picture of one who fights to not lose a sense of personal identity in exchange for group identity.

One challenge that many leaders of groups have is in developing relationships among members. For this reason, investing time in team building exercises or just groups activities can go a long way. Fortunately, there are tools a leader can use including mentorship, work structure, and leadership awareness to help improve the dynamics of a group or team.

A key part of leadership development is in having a mentor who is able to relate to the person being developed's current situation, their goals, as well as their challenges. This mentorship and ability to relate also goes a long way when trying to lead a group. Mentorship is a highly effective and well documented best practice for many successful organizations when done properly. It is important to pair someone with the right mentor who is be able to listen, understand, and provide useful feedback as well as opportunities for growth to the person they are mentoring.

Often people are tasked to serve on multiple teams in addition to the numerous individual tasks for which they are responsible. Taking time to reward and recognize members helps maintain morale. Rewards are typically motivating and although this book promotes inspiration over motivation, it is still recognized that motivation plays a role and can be very effective. Rewards can inspire others when they are truly earned and people can see why the person deserved the recognition.

If everyone is rewarded so that no one is left out then it is not really seen as anything special unless the entire group did something special. The reward becomes devalued in our minds and is uninspiring. It can in fact have the opposite effect, causing people to become cynical to the idea of rewards out of the perceived lack of value and sincerity behind the act which led to the reward of some while others worked much harder for the same reward.

In addition, leaders should provide an ample amount of efficient structure such that it is not laissez-faire nor highly directive. Leaders can also work to provide necessary resources and look ahead to anticipate potential organizational restraints that may impede either structure or effectiveness of the group. This way, a plan can be made in advance to address these challenges. These steps will prevent the unnecessary coordination loss of efforts of the members.

A responsible leader will also ensure that members are both competent and independently motivated in their performance to avoid motivation loss. This responsibility also extends to preventing ideology from poisoning the performance of group members. If your organization relies on the use of groups or teams to accomplish tasks then it behooves you to consider these concepts from Sociology.

Neuroscience

Neuroscience has been able to help explain that our brain is composed of three key parts: the cerebrum, the limbic system and the reptilian complex. The cerebrum is responsible for cognition and is only found in higher order mammals. This portion of the brain is responsible for tasks like reason and speech while the limbic system controls emotions and instincts such as eating, fighting, running for safety and reproduction. The reptilian portion of the brain, the oldest and most instinctual part of the human brain, is responsible for muscle control, balance, breathing, and heartbeat. What does this mean for leadership?

The intense pace of technological advances has caused the brains of leaders to become over stimulated. This is perfectly explained by Katharine McLennan of Mettle Group who wrote, "when the brain suddenly has to deal with the sixth decision after the fifth interruption in the midst of the search for the ninth missing piece of information on the same day that the third deal has collapsed, the brain begins to panic…" The transfer of information is no longer as slow as a phone call and the morning newspaper is considered out of date as soon as it is printed. With the rapid pace of information there is a constant push to have the most up to date information leading to inaccurate information which causes stress. Slowing down does not seem to be much of an option either. The problem is that leaders often make poor decisions under stress because under such stress the brain resorts to more primal instincts found in the reptilian complex. What then can be done?

Surprisingly the most effective ways to confront these challenges are quite old school. Meditation consistently ranks among one of the most effective ways of dealing with high stress. For example, Chi Gung (Qigong) is a Chinese meditation practice which dates back 5,000 years. It has been tested and proven to lower blood pressure, hypertension and other stress related symptoms. This practice typically involves remaining in a static position and taking long, slow, deep breaths. Meditation as a practice is found widely in many cultures. How is it that something so old is so relevant today?

The practice of meditation promotes positive physiological performance. By taking long, slow, deep breaths, the lungs are able to absorb more of the oxygen with each breath. This allows the oxygen to be pumped into the blood supply creating a higher level of oxygenation. This in turn allows more oxygen to be delivered to the brain via the blood stream. Slowing down the body's breathing rhythm also slows the heart rate causing the body to relax and become more calm. This is also aided with relaxing and extending the muscles of the body so that the body has good circulation. This entire process causes the body to not work as hard and allows the brain to enter a state very close to when it is asleep. All combined, meditation removes the stress from the prefrontal cortex and amygdala thus allowing it to return to a more normalized state. What does a leader with a brain performing well look like?

People tend to prefer working with and for those who are more positive and encouraging for a reason. Studies have found that for example, using a positive approach when coaching others stimulates the area of the brain involved with being open to new ideas and people. Charisma is a quality typically attributed to inspirational leaders. In particular, their visionary communication abilities play an important role. Just watch Bill Clinton as he gave the keynote at the 2012 Democratic National Convention to see what charisma looks like. There is research that suggests there is a neurological explanation for what is at play here.

When a leader forms and promotes a vision, it requires both a cognitive function and an emotional function. This means that there is integration taking place between different parts of the brain. Cognition is required to think of a direction and a desired outcome as is the case in coming up with a vision. This activity takes place in the cerebrum. Emotions must be kept in balance in order to positively promote the vision and be able to weather any negative responses from its promotion. This requires emotional regulation which is a function of the limbic system. What this means is that the greater a person's ability to cognitively formulate a vision and emotionally regulate their self so that they can successfully promote and gain support for their vision will as a result be a more inspiring and successful leader.

Organizational leaders are constantly inundated with tasks and challenges and therefore are most concerned with how the research of leadership and neuroscience can be applied. Luckily there are applications based on theory supported by research. For example, the prefrontal cortex which is the part of the brain responsible for higher order thought or executive functions, as in the case of deciding on making a large investment or working out a complex math problem, is only capable of performing this type of thought for short periods of time and as you become tired and your ability to effectively use this part of the brain diminishes.

What's The Difference?

The brains of men and women work differently because of adaptation. Ten thousand years ago most women performed mainly domestic activities including taking care of and raising children, looking after the place they lived and gathering useful items from the nearby area. A man's brain is more designed for hunting, fighting and reproducing. Where men have more than six times the amount of gray matter used for thinking, women have over nine times the amount of white matter which connects various parts of the brain giving each gender unique and useful tools.

Women are neurologically wired to understand language far better than men. A woman's brain is more sensitive to emotions and this makes sense if you are taking care of a baby that hasn't learned yet to speak. How do you know what the baby needs? Women are also more equipped for language. Women can use language to express emotions, develop relationships and be socially confrontational. This added sensitivity to emotion and built in wiring for language helps explain why so many women make great nurses, teachers and human resource professionals. These skills are found to be highly necessary in many leadership functions.

A man's brain is less sensitive to emotions and more designed for solving problems requiring logic and reason. It is not designed for language nearly as well as their female counterpart. This helps explain why militaries use simple and direct commands and have been very uniformed and rigid. Male brains are better designed for spatial awareness and navigation. The extra volume of *thinking* matter in the brain, increased ability to think logically and a reduced emotional sensitivity are all key factors in many management functions.

Men are in general larger and stronger than their female counterparts. This means they can exert more force over women and since they are the one who used weapons ten thousand years ago (and not much has changed since) they are able to use force to gain control. Women also have an innate desire to feel safe. This biological hardwiring has helped men be in dominant roles in most societies throughout human history although yes there have been a number of matriarchal societies. Of course there are women who can do advanced mathematics and men who are great communicators so it is not that when it comes to these factors it is all or nothing, it just means that each gender has a brain that has evolved for performing certain functions better than others.

As nations industrialized and increased their scale of production, they turned to an emerging set of management principles which took a mathematical look at how to optimize something like the way a factory operates. Academic researchers conducted studies to find the optimal use of resources and flow of work. By now you can probably tell that this was a very male driven initiative. Males almost exclusively ran businesses in the early days of management science and males almost exclusively went into academia so there was very little chance of getting anything other than a male oriented program.

What does all of this have to do with leadership? It helps us to understand the unique differences that people have. The better we understand a person's natural strengths and weaknesses we can then work to maximize that individual's output based on what the person is capable of and compelled to do and not based on a work flow chart. This method requires getting to know each person and therefore requires a bit more work up front. The payoff is well worth it when you consider that by doing so you are better able to connect the individual to the work they will be doing and will have fewer employee related problems over the long run.

The Future

Dr. Michio Kaku stated in an interview with Jon Stewart, "This is a golden age of brain research." There is a growing body of research being done in a new field of neuroscience called social cognitive neuroscience developed by Kevin Ochsner and Matthew Lieberman who defined it in 2001 as, "an emergent, interdisciplinary field that seeks to understand human interactions at the intersection of social, cognitive, and neural spheres of science." Social cognitive neuroscience is much broader than just the application of neuroscience to leadership; however, it does have application to leadership and professors from different universities and even the independent NeuroLeadership Institute conducts studies to find insights into leadership.

Leadership as a function is based largely on interactions with other people. These interactions are grounded in the way individuals think and feel about themselves then act as a result of those thoughts and feelings in relation to those around them and the organization. The more we can understand the workings of the brain such as which areas are more active during various leadership functions the better we can understand why someone is a more or less effective leader.

Researchers have found that the right frontal portion of the brain is more active in inspirational leaders and less active in non-inspirational leaders. This was found after conducting a study of 50 leaders who were tasked with describing future plans for their respective organization and to write a vision statement while undergoing a brain scan to see which areas were more or less active during the study. The researchers found that leaders who were considered more inspirational by their direct reports tended to write more socialized or communal vision statements and had heightened activity in the right front area of the brain. Those considered less inspirational by their direct reports wrote more individualized vision statements or became frustrated with the exercise altogether. The right frontal area of the brain was less active in the group of leaders.

The right frontal area of the brain appears to be an essential area to study with respect to leadership. This same area of the brain is also found to be key in effective interpersonal communication and social relationships. There is still a great deal of mystery locked inside the human brain. It is unknown exactly what controls or causes humans to experience consciousness or an awareness of themselves within the larger context. It is important however, to understand what is known about the human brain with respect to leadership and how that can be applied to enhance both current leaders and those being developed.

Psychology

Psychology is making an impact with the development of Emotional Intelligence (EI). EI refers to a person's ability to perceive, reason and regulate one's emotions. People are familiar with the idea of IQ or Intellectual Quotient, a person's score on a test that measures one's intellectual capacity. Unfortunately, success is not determined by intelligence. Much of leadership and management has to do with human interaction between superiors, co-workers, direct reports, customers, vendors etc. This simple fact makes it clear that it is important to be able to establish, build and maintain relationships with different types of people in different situations to be as effective as possible.

There is still more work to be done in developing Emotional Intelligence. For instance, there is no unified definition. Some scholars prefer to break the field of EI down into different parts and those parts are not always the same. There is also criticism around EI because it is extremely difficult to isolate EI skills and the development of those skills apart from other factors that may cause the same results. In spite of this, there is compelling research that shows that those with higher levels of EI perform more effectively as leaders and this has caused many organizations to support the implementation of EI training.

Even though there are multiple definitions of EI, the definition for EI embraced by many in the academic community is; "the capacity to reason about emotions, and of emotions to, enhance thinking. It includes the abilities to accurately perceive emotions, to access and generate emotions so as to assist thought, to understand emotions and emotional knowledge, and to reflectively regulate emotions so as to promote emotional and intellectual growth'. The definition breaks EI down into four parts: first, the ability to perceive emotion; second, the ability to integrate emotion with thought; third, understanding emotions; and fourth, the ability to manage emotions. By breaking emotional intelligence down into different pieces, each area can be measured independently and a more accurate assessment can be given.

An example of the four parts

A soldier returning from a combat tour in Iraq begins to have feelings of guilt, sadness, and feels generally negative about his life. The soldier's mother recognizes the behavior, realizing it is not the same as before the deployment. She notices increased drinking and a lack of drive or initiative in her son. The mother has so far completed the first part by being able to perceive the emotions and sees how they have manifested themselves in her son.

The mother now worried for her son, is conflicted. On the one hand she wants to help her son by possibly taking him to a therapist, but does not want to make her son upset at her to where he will distance himself from her too. She does not want to make him feel weak or unable to handle the challenges he is going through, yet does not want something bad to happen to him like crash his car while driving drunk or for him to commit suicide. She is not sure if she should leave him alone and hope things will work themselves out or possibly do something else. But do what? She is confused. This is the second piece, integrating emotions with thought, weighing conflicting emotions against each other while thinking rationally what to do.

The soldier drinks heavily, isolates himself and is prone to outbursts of anger. She recognizes that her son has signs of depression. When he talks he is pessimistic about his life and says he does not deserve to live. He mentions that it is not fair for him to be alive when he saw good people die. When asked to talk about it he thinks for a moment and then quickly leaves the room for several minutes before returning to say that he is ok when clearly he is not. The mother has now displayed the third element by labeling the emotions being displayed by her son as sadness and guilt, and understands these emotions are related to traumatic events he experienced while in combat.

The mother then decides she does not want to risk losing her son. Realizing it will most likely be very difficult, the mother tells her son how much she loves him and that although she doesn't know what happened she will help him get help so that he can learn to understand and overcome what he is going through. This is the fourth element, being able to regulate emotions in herself and make an effort to regulate the emotions in her son so that she can get him the treatment he obviously needs.

An alternate model

Another model for measuring and determining EI is one proposed by author, psychologist and science journalist Daniel Goleman. Goleman who published the ground breaking book Emotional Intelligence in 1995 and offers a definition and model more widely used by those in the non-academic community. According to him, emotional intelligence is defined as, "abilities such as being able to motivate oneself and persist in the face of frustrations; to control impulse and delay gratification; to regulate one's moods and keep distress from swamping the ability to think; to empathize and to hope". In his book, Goleman breaks EI down into five separate areas, three personal competence areas and two social competence areas. The five areas are as follows: one, self awareness; two, self-regulation; three, motivation; four, empathy; five, social skills.

An overriding theme in emotional intelligence is the recognition and regulation of emotions. The idea is that if a person is able to recognize and regulate his or her own emotions then that person has a sense of emotional discipline. This discipline comes in part from a self awareness such as understanding what actions trigger certain emotions or what behavior you naturally resort to when you are emotionally charged. The other part is the ability to blend critical thinking with emotion so as to not be led too strongly by emotion alone or on the other hand attempt to shut down your emotions and act purely from reason and logic.

A number of studies suggest that leaders with higher levels of EI perform better as leaders. One compelling example comes from Bell Labs which taught 600 engineering employees EI skills and after one year found productivity rise about 25% and a reported improvement in organizational climate. Another study found personality development, a result of higher EI, particularly in the areas of assertiveness, independence, optimism, flexibility and social responsibility separated a group of 51 high potential managers from a group of 51 regular managers who performed at an average level. Similar results have been found when performing studies to identify a link between EI and increased levels of leadership effectiveness. The more a person is able to regulate stress and emotions that can be negative while making a conscious effort to be open, optimistic, and willing to look at problems as challenges with an opportunity to learn and improve will show to have a higher level of leadership effectiveness.

The Golden Circle

The Golden Circle is a term coined by Simon Sinek and refers to his theory on how organizations should approach their reasoning for existence. Businesses are started out of a belief that there will be a profit earned. Because of this universal and obvious component, Sinek believes the idea of earning a profit should be forgone from a company's value proposition.

Sinek asserts that most organizations approach the big questions of an organization in reverse order of those who really make a mark in society and are the high achievers. The approach of coming up with what they do, how they do it and then why is the wrong order according to Sinek.

A fortune 500 company, religious group, nonprofit organization, governmental agency, weekly book club or any other group should instead ask first why, then how, then what. Profit for a business is the byproduct of getting those questions right, but not the core purpose which is why it should not be focused on as much.

START WITH WHY! Most groups have a mission and vision statement along with a list of core values, but how many people in the group really know what it is without reading it? Coming up with these things is supposed to be used as tools for creating a culture for the organization. If a group is to have a truly effective purpose then all people in the group should know its purpose because it has been internalized, not because they have been forced to memorize the one that management constructed. The Why question is what creates the vision of the group.

NEXT IS HOW! If you know that your organization's purpose is to build a community based effort to reduce carbon emissions then you have a vision and the next question is how. The how could be a mixture of creating awareness, holding events or reduction initiatives. Notice that these are more specific than the *Why* question but still lacking nuts and bolts. Now you have a mission.

LAST IS WHAT! This distinguishing factor is important because by working backward to conventional wisdom, the *What* question becomes fairly easy to put together. The local group aiming to reduce carbon emissions in their community could pass out literature that gives facts and information on how to get involved. Events could be held to answer questions, teach how to reduce emissions, and talk to people about the importance of grassroots movements. A community garden is just one example of a reduction initiative the group may adopt.

This method works so well according to Sinek because the main thrust behind all actions in the group are to reduce carbon emissions in the local community and that message is reflected in every action that is taken.

RQ Did anything in this chapter challenge the way you think about either your approach to management or leadership or the way you understand management or leadership?

RQ How can you apply The Golden Circle to your followers?

4. Creating a culture of inspiration

Inspiration is similar to most attempts to increase organizational morale or productivity in that if it is not maintained effectively the results will be lost over time. It is therefore important if a leader aims to achieve the powerful shift in making inspiration the accepted norm then a culture of inspiration must be created.

Imagine if an organization existed where every person arrived to work expecting to do their best because they want to do it for themselves and not because of an evaluation or other externally applied motivational technique. Imagine if there was such a culture that not only inspirational leadership was practiced but also inspirational followership. Think about the innovation, productivity, excitement, relationships and retention that would be possible in an organization such as this.

Inspirational leadership in its best form is not just practiced, but is a chosen lifestyle. The leader chooses to live an inspired life where in turn he or she is capable of being an inspirational figure at home, in social settings, and professionally. In doing so, the leader creates an opportunity to build a habit of being inspired by finding inspiration in everyday occurrences.

It is through this initiative to create an inspirational lifestyle that makes building an inspirational culture even possible because you understand it and have the experience necessary to be able to coach others in a similar direction. In the book The One Minute Manager by Ken Blanchard, the idea of catching people doing something right is highlighted. The idea is that too often managers look for employees that make mistakes and forget to encourage and support the ones who do the right thing. Showing recognition and appreciation is a simple way of leading toward a culture of inspiration, but it must be heartfelt and not said because you think that is what you are supposed to say.

One of the biggest pitfalls of a leader or organization that decides to establish a culture of inspiration is in not adequately planning how this will happen. Existing cultures do not change quickly. They are based on values, beliefs, and norms that a group has established, and maintained. In turn these may be tied to a leader, industry, religion, geography, ethnic culture or any other dynamic that can make change difficult.

Leadership Myths

It is important to look at some ideas about leadership that have developed over the last century, but as culture has changed some ideas have become more of a myth than reality. The first myth is that "leaders specify desired futures." The second myth is "leaders direct change." The third is "leaders eliminate disorder and the gap between intentions and reality." And finally the fourth myth of leadership is that "leaders influence others to enact desired futures." These are each ideal scenarios of how some think of leadership.

The truth is that leadership is hard. Not all people in a leadership role performs what some would consider leadership. Not all leaders have sufficient power and influence. Outside factors such as economics, civil unrest, or changes in technology can highly influence both power and influence. These ideas were born out of a time when people were trying to put organizations into the box of management that was developed throughout the 20th century. Anyone who has worked in management will attest that things at best sometimes, but more realistically rarely, go as planned.

The truth is that with the younger generation taking hold of the work force there is more demand for inclusion and collaboration than before. We have seen a rise over the last century in equality for a number of groups that have been marginalized including women and African Americans, and through that process have come to expect a sense of equality and justice. An overriding notion of leadership is that leaders influence others. This only happens if people buy into what you are trying to lead them toward. Increasingly people do not want to be led toward something. Instead, they want decisions to happen collaboratively so they feel they have a personal stake in the matter. Many people nowadays, myself included, look at a job, and more importantly the nature of the work they do, in context of how it impacts their careers and their lives as a whole. It is not just about having a job or receiving a paycheck. It's about creating a life you actually want.

It's pretty easy to see how each of these myths are truly just myth. If *leaders specify desired futures,* then less companies would fail, companies would have a staff of highly motivated employees who were experts at their job and companies would not end up in the news for questionable business practices. If *leaders direct change* then the President and other leaders could get Congress to eliminate the partisan politics that paralyzes real leadership from taking place. If *leaders eliminate disorder* then every employee would show up to work on time as intended instead of a few coming in late or calling in because "they are sick" on the Friday before a holiday weekend. If *leaders influence others to enact desired futures* then the leader would be able to win market share and customer loyalty from competitors.

Adaptive Work

Oftentimes management comes up with an idea after a meeting, conference, reading a book, or some other activity that gets them excited about a great idea they want to implement. There is a lot of enthusiasm initially and employees who have been exposed to this before are cautious at first and wait to see if the enthusiasm is sustained. More often than not the momentum for such initiatives dies out after a couple of months if it lasts that long. Why is that?

One big reason this exists is because often times leaders and managers are not properly educated in all facets of leadership or management; especially leading through change. A concept known as adaptive work pioneered by Harvard Professor Ron Heifetz, is one powerful tool taught by a number of scholars that emphasizes changing the entire culture of an organization and not one isolated piece. According to Heifetz, there is a difference between a more simple technical change and an adaptive change which involves changes in thoughts, behaviors, attitudes or culture.

Take for example the company that wants their staff to feel inspired, so they hire a speaker to come give a talk and get everyone excited. I bet you that most of the excitement created during the speech is gone within a week and what is left is gone in a month. A speaker, no matter how good they are, is not going to change an entire company's culture. C.E.O.s also do this where they will give a speech to workers to try to get them excited about a new vision, but without much follow through it doesn't go very far.

For an organization to really change its culture and become more inspirational they need to start with a conversation about their vision and core values. Is the organization's vision still the same? Has something changed that may cause the vision to need a makeover? What does each of the core values mean? Why *those* values? Are there others that may be more appropriate? Once questions like these have been thought about by each person, then discussed, and then reflected on, then discussed some more, can the group move on to the topic of inspiration. As you can see it is a lot of work that some organizations are unwilling to commit the time to completing.

The conversation about vision and values cannot be restricted to only top management either. It must include everyone from the very top to the very bottom. If everyone gets an honest say and holds similar beliefs then there is some pre-established buy in from the group as a whole. Too many times top management only allows themselves to be involved in deciding the vision and then decides to roll it out to everyone else. The result more often than not is management wondering why people aren't excited. HELLO! They didn't get a say in it.

Anyone that has been around children knows that if you give them a choice it works out much better usually than trying to dictate. The same goes for adults and especially line level employees. Management only makes a small percentage of an organization's total headcount; meaning that most of the work gets done by the workers. If the workers doing most of the work are given a say in what happens then usually positive results happen. Clearly if a few employees think it would be a good idea to have alcohol available in the cafeteria and these employees work at a school then it isn't feasible.

Fiat is an organization that understands this idea. People at any level are welcome to submit an idea that very well may be implemented. It does not matter how large or small the idea. This culture of openness breeds innovation as now you have an entire company that is able to come up with a new idea.

Google is another well known case of this type of collaborative innovation. Employees are allowed to spend twenty percent of their time working on projects not directly related to work. Some of their biggest successes such as Gmail have come as a result of allowing employees this creative freedom. If you want to continuously innovate in a fast changing market like technology, it is best if you activate as many of your people as possible.

If your employees are unhappy then their productivity wanes, they start showing up late or not at all to work, corruption tendency increases and overall organizational performance suffers. These are problems that no company wants, so give them a stake in the game and they will only be incentivized to give you a little more because they have a reason to now.

Next, the organization must figure out what role inspiration will play and how it will be deployed in order to have a chance at being effective, otherwise all you have are nice sounding words. Do you want people to be inspired to do quality work? Do you want them inspired to provide excellent service? Do you want them to be inspired to come up with innovative new ideas? All of these are possible if you have a good vision and mission with a core set of values that everyone both agrees on and is committed to.

This is where Simon Sinek's Golden Circle can come into application quite nicely. For the system, much the way process engineers design the best way to perform a process, there needs to be first a clearly understood reason why inspiration is the answer. Next, how will it be done and who is responsible for doing this? Finally, how will you know you have had success? This can be a tricky one. Measuring changes in productivity, absenteeism, workplace tension, retention, group cohesion, group satisfaction, and employee morale are some of the metrics that can be used as indicators for quantifying the effects. The good thing is that inspiration will be a by-product, just like profit, if you have a compelling mission and vision that people are truly committed to with the right leadership to get them there.

Sometimes the results you get are not what you were looking for, but they may be even better. Microwaves, lasers, and MRI technology all came as spin offs from the work that NASA did; but no one in NASA thought about a faster way to cook food when they worked on understanding microwaves. You must be careful though, changes in culture take time and people may not realize it right away that something is really changing so you must be persistent so you don't risk giving up on all the time and effort you had invested.

Examples

If a person or organization wants to create a real sense of inspiration it can be achieved in several ways. Having a charismatic leader that connects with people in a sincere personal way like Bill Clinton did during the second

Presidential debate in 1991 when he responded to a woman's question is one. That answer helped take Clinton from not being seen as a very formidable opponent to George H.W. Bush to becoming a person people saw as one that could relate to them, understand their concerns, and deal with them in a very real way. He also famously gained popularity with young people when he appeared on The Arsenio Hall Show and played *Heartbreak Hotel* on the saxophone.

Holding a special event aimed at inspiring others is another great way to stoke inspiration. Barack Obama used the 2004 Democratic National Convention as such a platform. At the time he was an Illinois State Senator and running for the U.S. Senate seat in Illinois. He was largely an unknown name before that event nationally, but after his appearance as the keynote speaker he became famous. He won the U.S. Senate seat he ran for and just four years later while still a freshman Senator, was elected the 44th President of the United States. Many others Senators and Congressmen have run for the Presidency and failed, often with significantly more legislative experience and national recognition.

Barack Obama and Bill Clinton did not win on singular events just as Apple did not become the largest company in the world with only one product. Abraham Lincoln is not known as one of the greatest U.S. Presidents to have lived solely for a single action. These feats were accomplished by a string of events taking place to build up to their eventual success.

Inspiration can be created several ways. Sometimes it is through a singular event or through an organized effort using a variety of methods. Regardless of how it is created, a key challenge is maintaining the level of inspiration over time and not allowing it to drift away as is commonly seen when inspiration is sparked by a singular event. This is why there is great need for inspirational maintenance.

To illustrate this point, let us look at the terrorist attack of September 11, 2001. Initially people were shocked, heartbroken, terrified, angry and full of questions. Within less than one month of the attack, American and British forces were laying siege on Afghanistan to go after the individuals responsible for carrying out such a heinous attack. 9/11 was the first attack on American soil since Pearl Harbor, the singular act which caused the U.S. to enter World War II.

Now with having been in Afghanistan and fighting for more than 12 years, and having simultaneously fought a second war in Iraq for eight years, the United States is less committed to the idea of fighting a war on terror. This is in part due to multiple reasons including reports that Iraq had very little to no connection to Al-Qaeda, that Iraq did not possess the weapons of mass destruction that a large part of the invasion was purported on, the cost of the two wars which has put the U.S. deep in debt, the loss of both military and civilian lives, and the fact that regardless of how many terrorists have been killed there are always more. Since 9/11 there have been no more successful terrorist attacks on U.S. soil. The point behind this example is that inspiration has a strong tendency to wane over time unless there are events to maintain the level of commitment.

So far inspiration and leadership have been discussed primarily in a positive light. It is possible however, to use propaganda and dishonest tactics to maintain inspiration for a cause. This unethical practice is not considered leadership by many. I point it out here because in the example of the 9/11attack the airplane hijackers were inspired to carry out the attack and kill innocent civilians. Conversely, the U.S. felt inspired to engage in a ground war in Afghanistan. This example illustrates how the inspiration of two separate groups can be conflicting and deadly.

Inspiration comes from things that seem big, daring, nearly impossible and then achieving them. This can be the reason why fighting against the last remaining superpower in the world which you see as evil according to your religious convictions is inspiring to some. It is also why Apple under the leadership of Steve Jobs was able to become the largest company in the world. Steve Jobs brought innovative ideas and vision. He shared those ideas with others. He only accepted the highest standard possible and he consistently delivered industry leading technology that left other companies gasping for air.

Each time Jobs would arrive on stage to reveal the latest Apple product in his trademark black turtleneck and blue jeans people were enthralled to see what it was. Lines out the door and record breaking sales became commonplace anytime a new product launch occurred regardless of the price. This all happened because Jobs understood how to maintain inspiration. He had a vision of creating incredible technology that was simple. The iPod does not have a bunch of buttons or switches; neither does the iPhone or iPad. This is much the same way that religious extremist groups have maintained the fervor for fighting that has endured regardless of how many troops we send or bombs we drop.

There are times when inspiration is needed to bring people together behind a singular act. Take for instance when President John F. Kennedy announced his intention to put a man on the moon within the decade during a speech given in 1961. This mission was driven by the space race with the Soviet Union who had taken the lead with Sputnik and with Yuri Gagarin being the first man in space. The space race was an extension of the Cold War that was at its height during the 1960's. The inspiration was created largely out of fear of losing the space race and the greater Cold War. It also served to build confidence in the young President and to bring citizens together with a renewed sense of nationalism.

Whether or not to use events to build and maintain inspiration and if so how, depends on practicality and necessity. Some companies use corporate retreats to take a group of people somewhere like Hawaii to go relax, hit up the golf course, eat good meals and hold meetings where people can discuss ideas or issues. These types of events can be very expensive between air travel, hotel accommodations, meals, guest speakers, entertainment and meeting room rental not to mention the time they are not doing their regular job. It may be too expensive for some to be practical. However, if people are spread out geographically then holding an event where people are brought together can be effective.

Some companies determine it is worth it to do these types of events because a retreat can allow people to refocus on why they are with the company and why they were chosen for their specific role in the company. It also allows for people to unwind so they can return to work more clear headed. These events can be great for getting people together who may not usually see each other very often. This way they can talk and build relationships with one another thereby creating a stronger bond within the company. Additionally, these events serve as a way to get people together usually in limited numbers so that a new vision can be launched and people are given a chance to buy in and offer up suggestions and concerns that can be addressed. When the people return back to their daily work they can share the new vision with others in an excited way and feel as though it is truly a shared vision and not one being forced upon them.

Signage is another tool that can help provide more regular day to day reminders of the vision. A great example of this are the motivational posters some people put up around offices that have a picture with a keyword and a saying or quote to go with it. For example a picture of a bald eagle with the word Excellence and the Aristotle quote, "We are what we repeatedly do. Excellence then, is not an act, but a habit". This could also be sticky note left on someone's computer that says 'Be your best,' or a banner that hangs in the entryway of an office that reads "Safety First" at a construction company. It is a good idea to create unique signs for your organization for originality sake.

Media is an effective method of maintaining inspiration in customers for businesses or people supporting a cause or movement. General Electric has put out commercials that highlight how the medical technology they create helps detect cancer earlier or has improved how a doctor can do his or her job. The Arab Spring was a time when social media was able to be used effectively. People were inspired by seeing the pictures and hearing reports from people on the ground at what was going on. Through Twitter and Facebook people were able to coordinate revolutionary attacks. In politics, talk radio is dominated by conservative talk show hosts like Rush Limbaugh, Sean Hannity and Glenn Beck who spend a majority of their show boosting a conservative agenda and making anyone not aligned with their beliefs look bad. They are able to fire up the conservative base, speak to millions of people on a daily basis, and promote conservative groups like the Heritage Foundation and Freedomworks thus guiding inspiration into action.

People may be the most significant form of maintaining inspiration in others because it is so personal. There is not as much meaning when a company airs a commercial that says, "We want to say thank you to all of our customers who have helped make our business a success over the past 25 years" or, "We have been proudly serving the community of Fredericksburg for 50 years." If someone comes to you, maybe puts their hand on your shoulder and says, "Tom, I've been really impressed with how well you have been doing your job. Your customers love to work with you. Thank you for what you do, you help make this company a success." That will carry significantly more weight because the individual sees they are recognized for what they personally do and that it is not only recognized but valued and communicated sincerely.

Personalized communication can really help someone want to do a good job even if they didn't really want to before because they see how much their manager cares for and appreciates them. That is the difference between inspiration and motivation. A motivator would say, "Tom, if you have the highest customer satisfaction score this month you can win a $50 prize." If he wins, the incentive is gone if it is not offered the next month. If he loses, a part of him will feel the extra effort was worthless because it didn't get him to the goal. By inspiring Tom, Tom does a better job because he wants to and not because of a prize or a goal.

It is important to point out that these methods are not guaranteed. They are tools that have potential. Again, what inspires some may not inspire all. It depends greatly on the organization's culture, the individuals within the organization and to what degree relationships have been developed. There are two important factors that must be kept in mind if these methods are to be used effectively. The first is to remember what makes something inspirational in the first place. The second is that ultimately you will have to figure out sometimes through trial and error and other times through a sense of the people what methods work best.

You may find that certain methods work better on certain individuals. Those with low self esteem will respond well with positive attention from their leader. Independently motivated people do not need as much personal attention and may find it distracting to their work and can be turned off by it. Signage and media are great forms, but those methods lose effectiveness if not changed often. The sign that is always there will be seen as just that, nothing different to be noticed or excited about unless it is something core that you want to stand the test of time. The same is true for making too many posts on social media or leaving too many encouraging notes or texts with people. Encourage people but respect their space and allow them the chance to do what you are trying to inspire them to do.

RQ What other examples of either individuals or organizations have you seen that have successfully created a culture of inspiration?

RQ What principles or commonalities can you find among these examples?

RQ How can you learn from these examples to improve your own effectiveness as a leader?

5. Inspirational Leadership During Times of Hardship

Inspirational leadership is a wonderful idea, especially when everything is going well. What about when things aren't going well? What about when they take a turn for the worse? How about when you receive terrible news or when tragedy strikes? Leadership can be extremely difficult. Everyone has an opinion of how it should be done yet most do not really want to be in the position to make the decisions and deal with the consequences of those decisions.

Hardship and tragedy raises questions. Questions that are often difficult to understand. Questions that may not have an answer or if it provides and answer, the answer appears to not provide any sense of hope or logic. Situations as these dig up painful emotions causing a person to question long held beliefs. At times these situations become the source of depression, alcoholism, violence, suicide or a sort of death and rebirth into a person with increased strength and wisdom. These times of extreme challenge are not a time to abandon inspiration rather, they are a chance to see the opportunity for inspiration contained within.

It is easy to lose inspiration during tough times. How can you imagine being inspired if your marriage just fell apart? If you suffer the death of a child? You are diagnosed with cancer? You lose your job? Your house burns down? It is possible to rise above such challenges.

Surely each situation is realistic. Surely it is easy to lose any sense of inspiration that previously existed. Surely it is also clear that if the sudden shock that follows creates a gripping sense of despair and feelings of hopelessness which if not overcome through a strong personal resolve will make the prospect of allowing inspiration in almost impossible. It is common to have feelings of denial, sadness, anger and hopelessness before coming to terms with the reality of the situation and being able to move forward from this stage of processing the situation.

Instead of becoming incapacitated by the onset of difficulty, recognize what can be done and begin quickly taking steps to gain whatever control of the situation possible. Understand that in times of great loss or great challenge that it is natural to have negative feelings. Therefore, there is no need to belittle yourself for only responding like a normal human being.

The most important fact to keep in mind is that everyone possesses the power of choice. It is only whether we take control of that tool or not which sets apart the successful among society from those who wallow in a consummation of despair. By taking control of the power of choice you must accept responsibility for the results of those decisions. Ask questions. The first question that is important to ask in troubling situations is whether anything can be done about it.

Viktor Frankl realized during his imprisonment in concentration camps during World War II that he had the power to not allow the humiliating acts he was required to perform break his human spirit. He realized that even if he couldn't change his condition he could choose how he responded to his condition. This act of strength became an inspiration to not just other prisoners but also the guards.

It is easy to be excited when everything is going well; if you just received a raise or your team surpassed a big goal it had set. Scenarios as these are not necessarily when inspiration is needed most. Rather, inspiration is oftentimes needed most during extreme difficulty. Life can sucker punch you when it appears to be going your way and then rob you of everything that defined you. It is during *these* times that inspiration is most often needed, and at times, most difficult to find.

A Personal Story

While serving a tour of duty in Iraq during 2005, one of my tasks was to assist in the mortuary when there were multiple casualties that needed to be processed. This duty was one I actually volunteered for surprisingly. Not out of a sick lust for death or the sight of bloody corpses, but because I was able to detach myself emotionally from the reality of what I would deal with. This was a skill learned through martial arts training and hardened during intense workouts and sparring sessions against more seasoned and larger opponents.

This task would prove to be the single most influential experience of the nine years I served in the military. The emotional detachment I thought I possessed turned out to be only temporary, not realizing that the psychological effects of experiencing a gruesome part of reality would catch up to me later. All of my training in martial arts and in the army had been simulated. There were never any life or death sparring matches; only controlled encounters of two people testing their will upon one another.

During that year of 2005 I assisted with a number of casualties. One person was thirty year old Staff Sergeant William Brooks who left behind a wife and two children in Alabama. His life was taken by an improvised explosive device or I.E.D. on May 3, 2005. Brooks is remembered as a fine soldier who many looked up to.

The loss of SSG Brooks left a family with no father and no husband. A mother and father who lost a son. A military unit who lost one of their own. Undoubtedly his presence is missed and his memory lives on as a great American.

Staff Sergeant Brooks was the first soldier that I would assist with in that year. His day of passing was just five days before my 21st birthday. He was someone I did not know personally though most likely I saw him in passing at the post office or out getting a bite to eat, but the memory of how I do remember seeing him is one I will never forget.

Another individual that stuck out particularly to me was that of a young soldier who served as a medic. He was Army Specialist Benyahmin Yahudah. His work was devoted to saving the lives of others. On the day of his passing 20 children lost their lives in the incident.

Part of what made the passing of this twenty four year old soldier stand out so much in my mind was what I found on him. While checking and logging his personal effects, the contents of everything he had on him, there were two items that really captured my attention. One was a Valentine's letter that he carried in one of his cargo pockets. Yahudah was killed July 7, 2005 making it clear that the letter was something he had been carrying for months with him everyday. The second item was a ring he wore bearing the inscription "true love waits".

Benyahmin Yahudah was a person described during his remembrance service by Brigadier General Ronald Silverman as one who "felt that saving lives was his calling." He was further described as a selfless and loving individual who enjoyed giving out toys and candy to children while out on patrol with his unit. Unfortunately an improvised explosive device embedded in a vehicle ended this young man's life and the lives of the 20 children who perished with him on that hot Summer day in Baghdad.

It was only a matter of days after returning from the deployment myself that I experienced my first panic attack. Triggered by the sight of ketchup mixed with scrambled eggs resembling the sight of human brains, I was launched into a full scale panic attack while eating breakfast at a Denny's restaurant with my mother. This was just before I was to be dropped off at the airport to go visit family in Oklahoma. This was not a positive way to begin my trip and left me terrified of what may later happen.

Completely blind-sided, I had no idea this would occur, had no idea how to react to it, and had no idea what else would come of it. The event completely terrified me as I tried to cover the sight of the eggs and rushed suddenly to the restroom in an effort to gather myself. Even as I write this I am on the verge of tears just revisiting the deep emotions this and other similar events would illicit.

The scariest part of the entire ordeal was that I did not know what would trigger these panic attacks and that once it started I was left defenseless. Unable to stop the attack from running its course, I was left vulnerable and terrified of what else lay in wait.

From then on I would have other encounters; once at an IHOP restaurant with my girlfriend at the time. She was scared so bad having never seen me go through one of these panic attacks that she called my mother to come get me. After I was taken home I laid in bed feeling numb wanting only to be left alone feeling both embarrassed and scared.

Questions would come up in my mind. Why did I live when other people died? Am I going to be able to get better? What else is going to happen? Even reading an article one night in an issue of Time magazine about a military unit returning home that mentioned how some of them didn't make it back alive caused me to break down into tears. One night while watching a movie with the same girlfriend I had to walk out because the movie triggered a panic reaction.

Thankfully I contacted a local Vet Center in San Diego and was placed with a fantastic therapist named Jane that I credit with honestly changing my life. She helped explain what was happening and why. She coached me through dealing with these situations when they came up. There was a sense of acceptance and understanding in her that made this all possible. Every day there are people just like Jane helping veterans wrestle with the challenges of Post Traumatic Stress Disorder.

I remember the intense emotional experience that came alongside answering questions about my life and recalling my time in the military. On one occasion after finishing my appointment with Jane I began to drive out of the parking lot and felt as though I was in a convoy in Iraq. I knew consciously that I was in San Diego but simultaneously I also felt the urge to be on the look out for snipers in windows, people walking with backpacks to conceal explosives, and debris near the curbs that could hide IEDs. This happened all the way until I exited the freeway in the area I lived on the outskirts of San Diego. It was as if I had pulled back into base and was in a safe zone.

As time went on I would learn how to reflect on what had happened and come to terms with it. Realizing that the unfortunate losses were permanent, I began to question the concepts of patriotism and freedom. It became clear how I would be able to honor those individuals the best way that I could.

Our fighting force is one made up of volunteers. This means there are individuals who choose to step out into harm's way if needed in order to protect others from having to. Marines, Soldiers, Sailors and Airmen do this to protect the freedoms of all Americans. They are the ones who provide the opportunity that America has to offer.

This meant that if I was going to honor these fallen brothers and sisters that I had to make a commitment that I would not waste the opportunities and freedoms that these brave souls protected by making the ultimate sacrifice. If they were willing to give their own lives for the sake of others who am I to just piss away the gift by only idly going throughout life. Why not maximize the power of the gift? Why not take advantage of the freedoms and opportunities that are afforded to us by the price these people made?

The main lesson of this story is that the human spirit makes it possible to come away with something positive after incredible difficulty. If we can do this with a sense of gratitude and passion to pursue something greater than ourselves then there is no reason we can not change the world. It is the difference between simply being alive and truly living. If these ideas are applied to leadership then one can not help but to feel inspired.

I should make it clear that I am in no way a psychologist or a psychiatrist. These are only lessons I have learned throughout my own life and wish to share with you.

Step By Step How To Have Inspiration In Times of Hardship

It is not expected that if someone were to lose a child, get divorced or have their house burn down that they would be able to just pick right up and move along. There are very real feelings of grief and sadness and heartache that occur and should be dealt with. The hope is that the following steps can simply be a guide for how to recover from such situations in a positive and healthy way. As the Theodore Roosevelt quote goes, "Do what you can, with what you have, where you are."

1. Can something be done about the situation?

This critical step is essential if you intend on being able to have a positive attitude in such challenging times. Also important, is to make full use of choices. It is important to remember that everyone makes a choice even if the choice is not to make a choice. There has only been a choice in this instance to push the decision to a later point or allow other conditions to dictate the choice for you. If you do this you have no reason to complain of the outcome for you left it to other circumstances to decide the choice on your behalf.

Unfortunately it is often natural and easy to fall into the victim mentality. People are empowered when they feel in control of their lives. This starts by taking control of the situations we are in every day. What do you want for your life? What will you accept? Is this challenge so big that it will break your spirit? It was Friedrich Nietzsche who wrote, "He who has a strong enough why can bear almost any how."

2. Once we accept that which we cannot change we can then focus on what can be done.

At times people find themselves in tremendously difficult situations that seem unimaginable. And while these situations may be horrific, it is vital to focus on what can be done in that situation. It is unfortunate when people are thrust into terrible circumstances in which they have seemingly no control over, but the reality is that it happens. The real question is not *if* it will happen, or even *when* because we already know that it will. The real question, the one that is most telling is, *what will you do*? Will you give up and quit or will you rise above the devastation?

Harriet Tubman was unable to eradicate slavery. It would have been easy for her to throw her hands up and say "to hell with it". Instead of focusing on what she could not change, she chose to focus on what she could. She would go on to lead many people to freedom through her underground railroad. She brought hope to countless individuals as she rescued over 300 slaves and was proud of the fact that she "never lost a single passenger." All of this came from a woman who was born into slavery and never learned to read or write. Tubman is a perfect example of someone who focused on what could be done instead of making excuses about why it couldn't be done.

3. Some things may be bad now so choose to focus on the good that can be achieved in the future or the good that was achieved in the past.

A positive attitude is the friend of inspiration. If a loved one is lost it is extremely difficult to focus on nothing but the pain and sadness such an event causes; especially so when it happens to a child. It is helpful to concentrate on the good parts of the life that person experienced. It is also a time of reflection that reinforces in the heart of those affected that each day is a gift that should not be wasted. For we have a day that others are unfortunate to not experience; so experience it the best you can.

Groups like the Wounded Warrior Project and Make a Wish have been created under the vision of recognizing the unfortunate reality that people deal with and do something to improve the lives of these individuals. This is a fantastic example of a group of people taking a bad situation and seeing what good can be accomplished in the future and then making meaningful and realistic steps to do something positive. There are countless other individuals and groups out there making a difference. What difference will you make?

The first place to start with when changing a bad situation into a good one is your attitude. This also means taking responsibility for your attitude, the choices you make and the success and failures of your conviction. There are many examples of individuals going beyond what is considered *normal* to achieve unbelievable outcomes. One incredible example is that of Buddhist monk Thich Quang Duc who set himself on fire on a busy street in Saigon on June 11, 1963 in protest of the South Vietnamese government. A photo of the incident hit headlines worldwide and President Kennedy remarked on the photo saying, "No news picture in history has generated so much emotion around the world as that one." Thich Quang Duc is an example of someone who held extreme devotion to his belief as he sat in a meditative posture while his body was consumed by flames.

By only choosing to accept what life gives you, it becomes easy to absolve yourself of the responsibility for your condition.

4. Find a healthy positive way to honor lost love ones.

There are many fantastic ways people have done this. One way is to leave an empty chair and place setting at the table during Thanksgiving for someone as a way to remember them.
Another great ways is through the use of photos, possibly creating a remembrance area like is common in many Asian cultures to have of their ancestors.

Continue to celebrate special days in their life. If the person was your husband or wife you can continue to celebrate the anniversary by going to dinner and writing an anniversary card to your lost spouse. Birthdays or the day they passed are also ways people choose to celebrate by putting flowers on their grave site or by doing activities that person enjoyed coupled with a time of memory sharing.

RQ Think back on your experiences of confronting hardship and consider how these ideas may have helped through this time of difficulty.

RQ Are there any other ways you have found that safely and effectively help when leading through hardship?

6. Inspiring Yourself: When is inspiration useful, necessary and why?

This can perhaps be the most difficult part of inspirational leadership. If you remember from the very beginning, there was a simple definition of leadership written that says, "Leadership is the act of leading." You are a person and you can lead yourself. Often times we look to others as a source of the inspiration. We watch movies, listen to music, and read inspiring quotes or search out for anything else we can find to be inspiring. Why not inspire yourself?

Yes this may be the most difficult part of inspirational leadership, but it may be the most important part as well. It has been said that you do not need to be in a leadership role to be a leader. Martin Luther King Jr. was not elected or appointed to be the great civil rights leader that he was. Somewhere along the way he chose to become the great civil rights leader that he was and others supported his vision and believed in him. He understood that a great deal of work had to be done and that he could choose to be a part of the solution or to hide in the shadows avoiding trouble by not speaking or acting out. As time went on, he saw bits of progress and others joined. He was able to look back at his accomplishments and be inspired by himself, by what he had done.

This ability to choose a cause then work toward that cause, realizing it will and should be difficult is key. You learn to fight for every step. You choose every time you are faced with adversity to give up and quit or to keep going. As you struggle on, you are encouraged by the strength of your resolve. As you forge through the challenges you face, you earn small victories along the way. Being able to look back at what you have been able to accomplish in the name of your chosen cause, by your own choice, of your own resolve, is what inspires you to drive on. This is how you inspire yourself.

Lau-Tzu wrote in his book Tao Te Ching, "A journey of a thousand miles begins with a single step". No one would remember the quote if it read, "the journey to the bathroom begins with a single step". Again, the element of something big, daring and almost impossible is what is inspiring. No one is inspired by you living your life in mediocrity, not even you. One of my personal heroes, Theodore Roosevelt, wrote in his autobiography, "With gentleness and tenderness there must go a dauntless bravery and grim acceptance of labor and hardship and peril." How can you possibly expect to be inspiring to yourself or others if you accept mediocrity?

Follow your passions. That is the easiest way to start. When people fail at doing something it is typically a result of the following: you were not that committed to the idea in the first place, when it became difficult you quit, you looked for reasons to call it a failure without giving it a real chance, you did not believe in yourself, you were afraid to fail.

Most people are afraid to fail. This applies to all areas of life. People are afraid to speak in public out of fear they will mess up or be laughed at. There would have been no "I Have a Dream" speech if Martin Luther King Jr. thought that way. People are afraid of being rejected and don't ask for that raise they think they deserve. People are afraid of being ashamed to admit they are not happy in their relationship so they stay together miserably living a lie. People are afraid of not earning enough money and go to college and take jobs doing things they are not interested in just because it might pay well. There are others and using reasons like these are horrible ways to live your life. It is uninspiring and who wants that?

Take a lesson from Gandhi who wrote "When I despair, I remember that all through history the way of truth and love have always won. There have been tyrants and murderers, and for a time, they can seem invincible, but in the end, they always fall. Think of it always." Gandhi was not a large man, he did not command an army nor did he choose to use force against his oppressors. Rather, he used non-violent civil disobedience. He, through his courage and actions, inspired others who followed in his example to stand up to the British empire for Indian independence. He was later assassinated for his beliefs and has become recognized as one of the most inspiring leaders in not just the 20th century, but in all of history.

Self Inspiration Demonstrated By Arnold Schwarzenegger

In 2010, Arnold Schwarzenegger gave the keynote address at Emory University. During the commencement speech Schwarzenegger took the time to explain his six secrets to success that he says have led him to the many outstanding accomplishments a man of his background was not so easily able to accomplish.

Schwarzenegger was born and grew up in Austria. His father was a police officer and would have been happy to see his son grow up to be one himself or something similar. When a teenage Schwarzenegger got the idea to become a championship bodybuilder. His family thought he was crazy.

1) **Trust Yourself**: Arnold decided to take bodybuilding serious as a teenager. He was not content with simply following the sport or participating as a novice. He decided to become a champion. By the time he was 18 he was already training three hours per day in addition to a full days worth of military training. The first competition that Arnold competed in was the Junior Mister Europe and he won first place. This would only be the beginning for Arnold Schwarzenegger who would go on to have a successful career in bodybuilding, acting and politics.

2) **Break The Rules**: In order to compete in the Junior Mister Europe competition he left his military base that he was assigned to without permission, traveling from Austria to Stuttgart, Germany. Arriving by train the day of the event, Schwarzenneger actually used trunks from another competitor who had already competed because he did not have his own.

3) **Don't Be Afraid To Fail**: Though he admits having doubts about whether he should have left the base at the time, he understood that he would soon be 18 and too old to compete in the junior competition. The punishment for leaving without authorization would be severe if it was discovered he had left. This did not stop Arnold who went past the fear of failure and won the first bodybuilding competition he ever entered.

4) **Don't Listen To The Naysayers**: Schwarzenneger has heard the voices of many naysayers throughout his storied career. Fortunately for not only himself, but for all of those inspired by his accomplishments, he did not listen to them, he listened to himself. From his parents telling him it was silly to pursue bodybuilding, to agents laughing at him about the idea of getting into acting, and then later people doubting his ability to become Governor of California.

Arnold is not content with only doing something great. He wants to do it BIG. He wants to prove to himself and to others who doubt him that he can be successful in more than just one venture.

5) **Work Like Hell**: Having been discovered for leaving the base to attend the competition he was prepared to be in deep trouble. However, the word spread that he won the competition. Quick to take advantage of the opportunity, Arnold gave the credit to his leaders for all of the great training he received from them. Knowing they had to do something, they assigned him to work in the kitchen as punishment peeling potatoes. In actuality they used it as a way to feed him more in order to fuel his training needs.

His military leaders made sure he had time to train and his regimen increased to five hours per day after his regular work duties. Later he would go on to win the Mister Universe title at the age of 20, the youngest person to do so. He would go on to win that competition a total of 5 times along with seven Mister Olympia titles.

The hunger for accomplishment did not end with bodybuilding. Emboldened by what he had already achieved, Schwarzenegger set his sights on Hollywood. Again, acting agents told him it would never work out. At the time, Arnold was trying to break into the acting scene, the big names in Hollywood were smaller guys like Dustin Hoffman, Al Pacino and Woody Allen. He was teased about his accent and his awkward name.

Determined to improve his skills just as he had done in bodybuilding, Schwarzenegger applied the discipline and drive he had developed into his acting. He began taking classes on everything from developing accent to removing his own accent as well as others.

6) **Give Back**: Upon deciding to run for Governor of the State of California, Schwarzenegger was told that you don't just go straight for the top job like that. Instead he was told to run for lower offices and work himself up over time. He told these people that he was not interested in being a politician, but that he wanted to be Governor to give back to the State that had given him so much over his career. As Governor he did not accept a paycheck.

Arnold who is now in his sixties continues to put out movies while being involved in events and activities to help tackle global issues. Arnold continues giving back by raising awareness and money for the After-School All Stars program which he helped create.

Everyone knows someone who seems to have "the good life." The person who is always in a good mood, the one who travels, goes out to parties, and has a good job. When you realize that was entirely by choice and not consequence, and that you too can have that if you choose, then you are on your way to an inspiring life.

What inspires me

So far I have written to explain just about everything there is to know about inspirational leadership. I would like to share with you some of the things that inspire me. I think it is important because it allows you the reader to connect a bit deeper with me as a person. I also believe it's important to be aware of what inspires you so maybe understanding what inspires me and why can help you if you don't understand just yet.

I am inspired by the idea that in no organization do people complain of too much leadership in the same way that people complain of too much management. That is the central idea behind why I am so interested in the study of leadership. Nobody goes to their boss and says "Excuse me, can you be less supportive? Can you not be quite so visionary? Would you mind being less passionate about what we are doing because it is making me enjoy my job way too much? Maybe instead you could come up with some more rules or policies or when was the last time we updated the employee handbook?" It is an idea like this that helps define the difference between leadership and management and reinforces the reason leadership is so important.

I stumbled upon another insight that has deeply inspired my push for inspirational leadership. As I sat back and thought of the great leaders throughout history and realized that no one refers to them as motivating managers, but that everyone refers to them as inspiring leaders I knew I had hit on something. I contemplated Jesus Christ, Mohandas Gandhi, Nelson Mandela, Martin Luther King Jr., Abraham Lincoln, Oprah Winfrey, Harriet Tubman, Malala Yousafzai, Michael Jordan and Muhammad Ali quickly realizing they all had parallels in their stories. People understand the difference, and choose to hold high in society the ones who inspire and lead instead of the ones who motivate and manage.

I am also inspired by highly passionate people who are very good at what they do. I have watched hours of Youtube videos with Neil De Grasse Tyson because he has a deep conviction for the need to support the exploration of space. He understands that he is in a position to advocate for being scientifically literate. He speaks about the value that NASAs work has contributed to society among many other ideas.

Tony Hsieh and Seth Godin are other examples of people by which I am inspired. Hsieh is CEO of Zappos, ranked several times as one of the best companies to work for, and author of the book Delivering Happiness. Hsieh has developed a company culture based on doing the exact opposite of what has been the standard in companies for more than a century, making people happy. Seth Godin is an author and blogger who promotes the idea of making your life a work of art where you put yourself into everything that you do and not settle for doing a job because it's just a job and you need to pay your bills. He encourages people to fill their lives with a sense of living and not mere existing.

Perhaps the one thing that most inspires me is the fact that it is possible to build and develop inspiring leaders who can change the world in a positive way. It is my calling to be one of these people who changes the world by empowering leaders with the knowledge and tools needed to be successful.

RQ Are there any "rules," principles, mantras or ideas that you use to inspire yourself?

RQ Part of being a great leader is helping develop others, what do you plan to take from this book and share with others in order to make them not only better followers or future leaders, but more importantly better individuals?

Bibliography

Ahmad, Z. (2010). Brain in business: The economics of neuroscience. *The Malaysian Journal of Medical Sciences, 17*(2), 1-3.

Aparna Joshi, M. B. (2009). Getting everyone on board: the role of inspirational leadership in geographically dispersed teams. *Organization Science Vol. 20, No. 1*, 240-252.

Ashkanasy, N. M. (2013). Neuroscience and leadership: Take care not to throw the baby out with the bathwater. *Journal of Management Inquiry*, 311-313.

Avolio, B. J. (2004). *The encyclopedia of leadership.* Thousand Oaks: Sage Publications Inc.

Balthazard, P., Waldman, D., Thatcher, R., and Hannah, S. (2012). Differentiating Transformational and non-Transformational leaders on the basis of neurological imaging. *The Leadership Quarterly*, 244-258.

Barker, R. A. (1997). How can we train leaders if we do no know what leadership is? *Human Relations Vol. 50, No. 4*, 343-362.

Blake, A., Strozzi-Heckler, R., and Haines, S. (2013). Somatics, neuroscience, and leadership. Retrieved from http://www.strozziinstitute.com.

Boyatzis, R. (2012). Neuroscience and the link between inspirational leadership and resonant relationships. *Ivey Business Journal*.

Buffett, Warren (1998). Buffett and Gates on Success. Salient Media

Burns, J. M. (1978). *Leadership.* New York: Free Press.

Center for Disease Control, MMWR (1999, April 2). Achievements in public health, 1900-1999 impact of vaccines universally recommended for children-United States, 1990-1998. MMWR Weekly 48 (12) pp.

243-248. Table 1. Retrieved from http://www.cdc.gov/mmwr/preview/ mmwrhtml/00056803.htm#00003753.htm

Chopra, P. K., and Kanji, G. K. (2010). Emotional intelligence: A catalyst for inspirational leadership and management excellence. *Total Quality Management*, 971-1004.

Del Jones and, M. K. (2007, Jan 04). Home depot boots CEO Nardelli ; he arrived when company was hot, but he didn't make it hotter. *USA TODAY*. Retrieved from http://ezproxy.nu.edu/login?url=http:// search.proquest.com/docview/408971515?accountid=25320

Eddings, J. (1993, August 30). `I have a dream'--30 years ago and now. *US News and World Report*, *115*(9), 10.

Eversley, M. (2011, April 11). Harriet Tubman changed the world with bravery. *USA Today*, p. 15.

Frankl, V. (2000). *Recollections: An autobiography*. New York, NY: Purseus Publishing.'

Goethals, G., Sorenson, G., Burns, J., & Luker, R. (2004). King, Martin Luther, Jr. (1919-1968) In G. Goethals, G. Sorenson & J. Burns (Eds.), *The encyclopedia of leadership*. Thousand Oaks, California: SAGE Publications, Inc.

Goethals, G., Sorenson, G., Burns, J., & Strock, J. (2004). Roosevelt, Theodore (1858-1919). In G. Goethals, G. Sorenson & J. Burns (Eds.), *The Encyclopedia of leadership*. Thousand Oaks, California: SAGE Publications, Inc.

Golnaz, S. (2012). Emotional intelligence and leadership development. *Public Personnel Management*, 535-546.

Home alone; corporate governance. (2007, January 6). *The Economist*, 54.

Houglum, D. T. (2012). Myth-Busters: Traditional and emergent leadership. *E:CO Issue Vol. 14 N0.2*, 25-39.

Hughes, Langston (1994). Mother to Son (First published 1922). The Collected Poems of Langston Hughes. The estate of Langston Hughes. Random House

Julie-Anne Sheppard, J. C. (2013). Twenty-first century leadership: international imperatives. *Management Decision Vol. 51, No. 2*, 267-280.

Kaiser, Robert B., J. L. (2012). The how and what of leadership. *Consulting Psychology Journal: Practice and Research Vol. 64, No. 2*, 119-132.

Kaku, M. (Performer) (2014). Tuesday February, 25 [Television series episode]. In Stewart, J. (Executive Producer), *The Daily Show*. New York: Viacom. Retrieved from www.thedailyshow.com

Kanji, P. K. (2010). Emotional intelligence: A catalyst for inspirational leadership and management excellence. *Total Quality Management*, 971-1004.

Kathryn Burleson, C. W. (2005). Upward social comparison and self-concept: Inspiration and inferiority among art students in an advanced programme. *British Journal of Social Psychology*, 109-122.

King Jr., Martin Luther (1963, August 28). I have a dream. March on Washington. Washington D.C.

Kiyosaki, Robert (1997). Rich Dad Poor Dad. Warner Books

Kussrow, P. (2001). Brain-based leadership. *Contemporary Education*, *72*(2), 10-14.

Lee, N., and Chamberlain, L. (2007). Neuroimaging and psychophysiological measurement in organizational research: An agenda for organizational cognitive neuroscience. *Annals of the New York Academy of Sciences*, 18-42.

Levy, S. (2011, November). Steve jobs. *The Atlantic.*

McGill, S. (2005). Harriet Tubman. *Harriet Tubman*, 1.

Roosevelt, T. (1913). *Theodore Roosevelt; an autobiography*. New York: MacMillan.

Obama, Barack (2011, July 12). Congressional Medal of Honor Ceremony. White House, Washington, D.C.

Ochsner, K. N., & Lieberman, M. D. (2001). The emergence of social cognitive neuroscience. *The American Psychologist*, 717-734.

Pace, A. (2012, December). Brain-based learning for leaders. *Training and Development*.

Phenomenal Oprah spoke across barriers. (2011, May 7). *State News Service.*

Politico.com (2012). 2012 Presidential Election. Retrieved from http://www.politico.com/2012-election/map/#/President/2012/

Ringleb, A., Rock, D., & Ancona, C. (2012). NeuroLeadership in 2011 and 2012. *NeuroLeadership Journal*, 1-35.

Roberts, S. (2005, November 4). 1955: moving to the front of the bus. *New York Times Upfront.*

Rock, D. (2010). *The neuroscience of leadership*. (Doctoral dissertation).

Roosevelt, Theodore (1910, April 23). Citizenship in a republic. Paris, France.

Roosevelt, Theodore (1912, October 14). Milwaukee Wisconsin.

Sadri, G. (2012). Emotional intelligence and leadership development. *Public Personnel Management Vol. 41 No. 3*, 535-545.

Schwarzenegger, Arnold (2010, May 10). Commencement Address, Emory University

Senior, C., Lee, N., and Butler, M. (2011). Organizational cognitive neuroscience. *Organization Science*, 804-815.

Silver, Nate (2013, January 23). Contemplating Obama's Place in History, Statistically. fivethirtyeight blog. New York Times. Retrieved from http://history-statistically/

Sinek, Simon (2009, September). How great leaders inspire action. Tedx

The Neuroleadership Institute. (2013). Retrieved from Neuro Leadership: www.neuroleadership.org.

Time for inspirational leadership. (2012, October 22). *The Indianapolis Business Journal*.

Towards inspirational leadership. (2008, September). *The Lamp*, 19.

Tzu, L. *Tao te ching*. Publish date unknown.

Waldman, D., Balthazard, P., & Peterson, S. (2011). Leadership and Neuroscience: Can we revolutionize the way that inspirational leaders are identified and developed? *Academy of Management Perspectives*, 60-74.

Waldman, D., Balthazard, P., and Peterson, S. (2011 b). Social cognitive neuroscience and leadership. *The Leadership Quarterly*, 1092-1106.

Xie, J. (2013, June 10). *June 11, 1963*. Retrieved from http://www.politico.com/gallery/2013/06/june-11-1963/001093-015407.html

Yousafzai, Malala, (2013). I Am Malala: The girl who stood up for education and was shot by the Taliban. Orion House.

www.ingramcontent.com/pod-product-compliance
Lightning Source LLC
Chambersburg PA
CBHW071612170526
45166CB00003B/1064